PIANO • VOCAL • GUITAR

CHART HITS

OF 2020-2021

ISBN 978-1-70513-409-2

HAL•LEONARD®

Visit Hal Leonard Online at
www.halleonard.com

Contact us:
Hal Leonard
7777 West Bluemound Road
Milwaukee, WI 53213
Email: info@halleonard.com

In Europe, contact:
Hal Leonard Europe Limited
42 Wigmore Street
Marylebone, London, W1U 2RN
Email: info@halleonardeurope.com

In Australia, contact:
Hal Leonard Australia Pty. Ltd.
4 Lentara Court
Cheltenham, Victoria, 3192 Australia
Email: info@halleonard.com.au

CONTENTS

AFTERGLOW

Words and Music by ED SHEERAN,
DAVID HODGES and FRED GIBSON

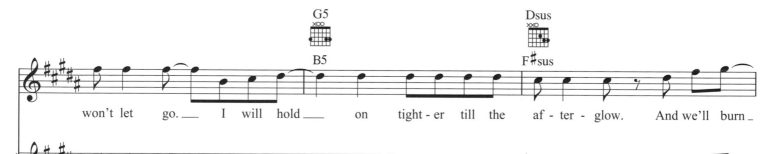

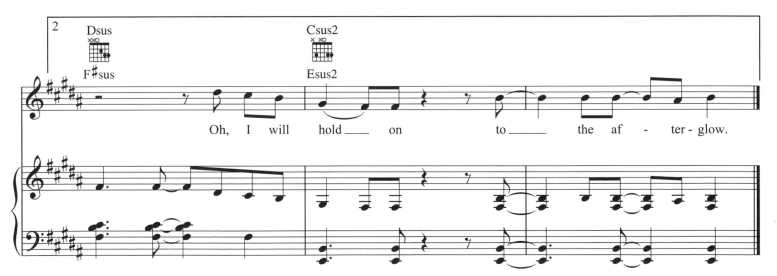

ANYONE

Words and Music by JUSTIN BIEBER,
JON BELLION, JORDAN JOHNSON,
ALEXANDER IZQUIERDO, ANDREW WATT,
RAUL CUBINA, STEFAN JOHNSON
and MICHAEL POLLACK

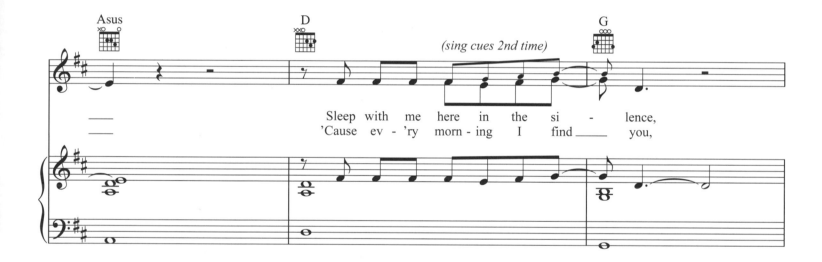

pre - dict the fu - ture, so just hold on like you will nev - er let go. _____
pre - dict the fu - ture, 'cause cer - tain things are out of our con - trol. _____

Yeah,

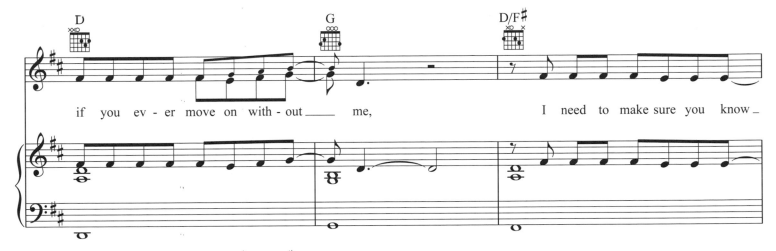

if you ev - er move on with - out _____ me, I need to make sure you know _____

that you _____ are the on - ly one _____ I'll ev -

er love. (I got - ta tell you, got - ta tell you.) Ee - yeah, you, _____ if it's not _____

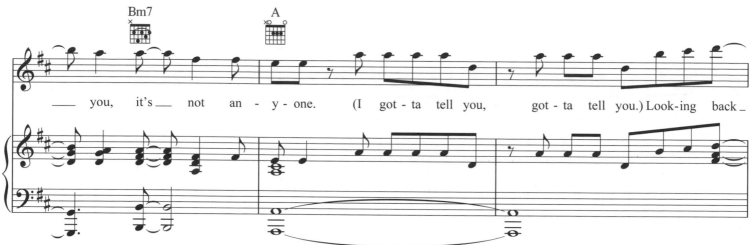

you, it's __ not an - y - one. (I got - ta tell you, got - ta tell you.) Look - ing back __

__ on my life, __ you're the on - ly good __ I've ev - er done. (Ev -

er done.) Ee - yeah, you, _____ if it's not __ you, it's __ not an -

y - one. (An - y - one.) Not an - y - one.   y - one. It's not __ an - y-

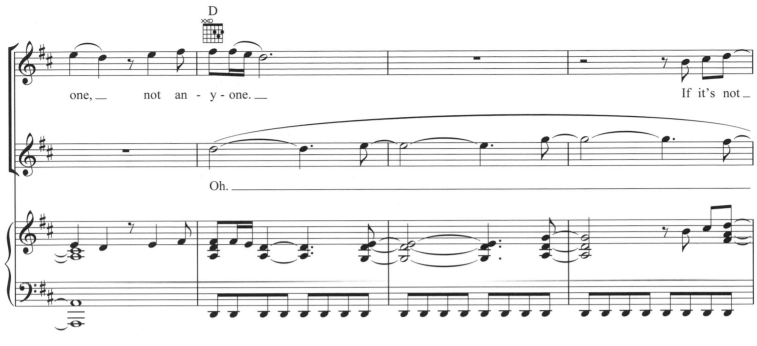

one, _ not an - y - one. _

Oh. _____

If it's not _

_____ you, it's _ not an - y - one.

Oh, _ yeah, _____ whoa. _

Oh. _

Ee - yeah, you _____ are the on - ly one _ I'll ev -

er love. (I got-ta tell you, got-ta tell you.) Ee-yeah, you, _____ if it's not _

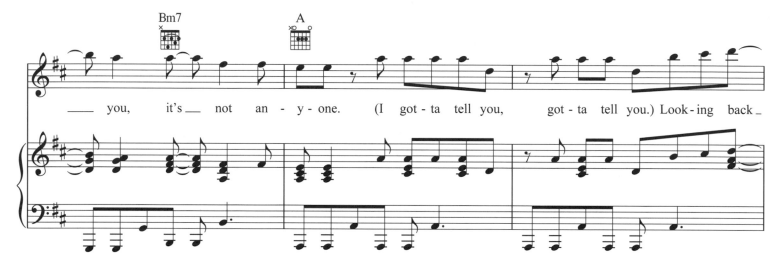

_____ you, it's _ not an-y-one. (I got-ta tell you, got-ta tell you.) Look-ing back _

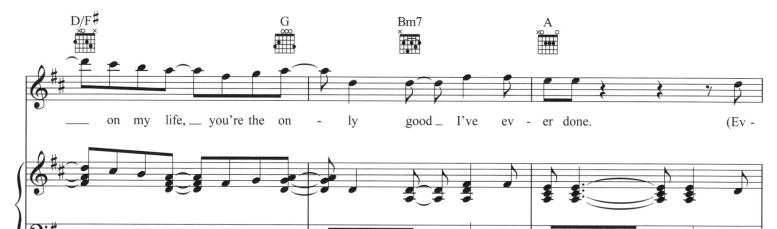

_____ on my life, _ you're the on - ly good _ I've ev - er done. (Ev -

er done.) Ee-yeah, you, _____ if it's not _____ you, it's _ not an-y-one.

BANG!

Words and Music by ADAM METZGER,
JACK METZGER and RYAN METZGER

I get up, ___ I get down ___ and I'm jump - in' a - round. ___ And the rum -

- pus and ruck - us are com - f'ta - ble now. ___ Been a hell of a ride, ___ but I'm

think - in' it's time ___ to grow. ___ Bang, bang, bang! So, I got ___

_____ an a-part- ment a-cross _____ from the park. _____ Put qui- noa _____ in my fridge, _____ still I'm not _____

_____ feel- in' grown. _____ Been a hell of a ride, _____ but I'm think- in' it's time _____ to go. _____

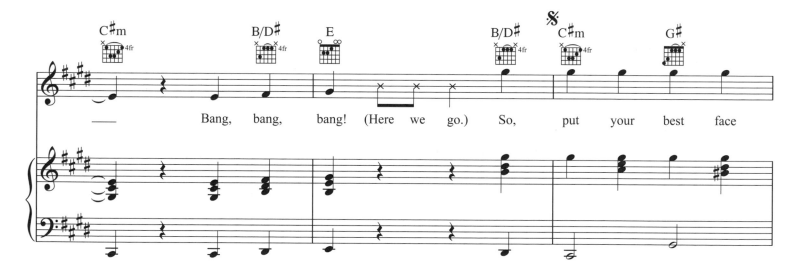

_____ Bang, bang, bang! (Here we go.) So, put your best face

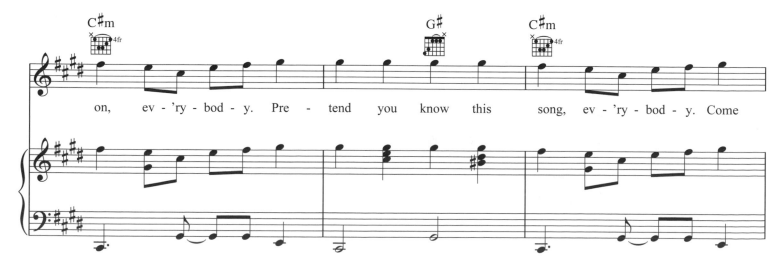

on, ev- 'ry- bod- y. Pre - tend you know this song, ev- 'ry- bod- y. Come

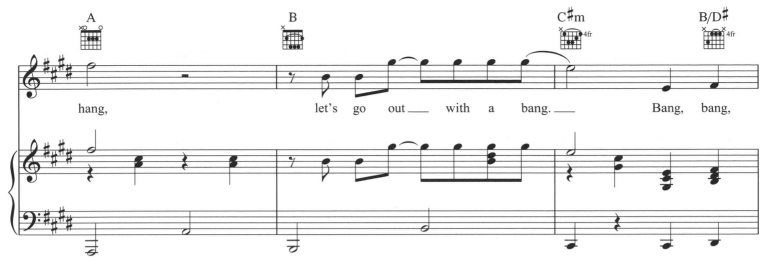

hang,   let's go out ___ with a bang. ___   Bang, bang,

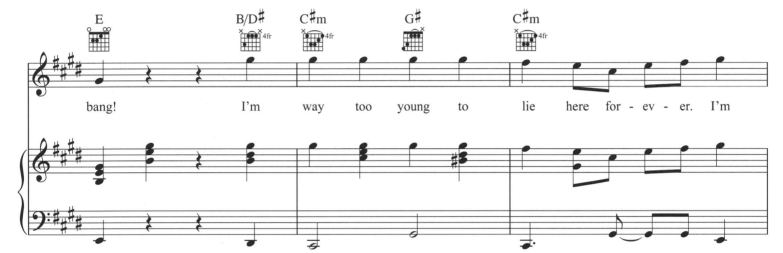

bang!   I'm way too young to lie here for - ev - er. I'm

way too old to try, so what - ev - er. Come hang,

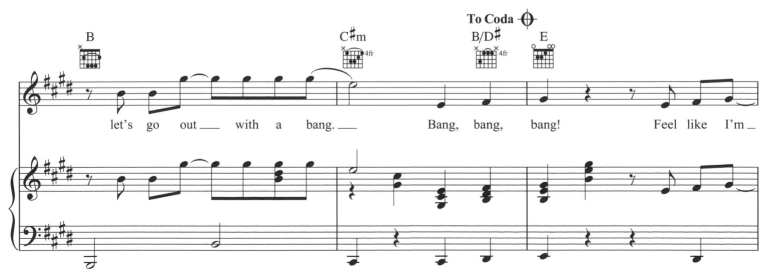

let's go out ___ with a bang. ___   Bang, bang, bang!   Feel like I'm ___

___ gon-na puke ___ 'cause my tax ___ - es are due. ___ Do my pass - word be-gin ___ with a one ___

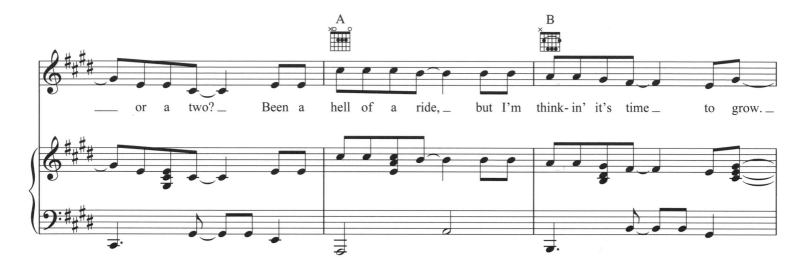

___ or a two? ___ Been a hell of a ride, ___ but I'm think-in' it's time ___ to grow. ___

___ Bang, bang, bang! (Met - ro - nome.) Man, I'm up to some -thin'.

Ooh de la de do. Thank you all for com - in'. I hope you like the show, 'cause it's

on a bud-get. So, ooh de la de do, yeah. Come on, here we go, yeah.

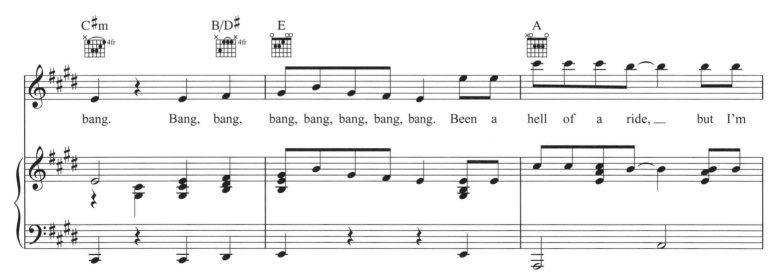

Come on. (Here we go.) So,   bang, bang, bang, bang, bang,   bang,

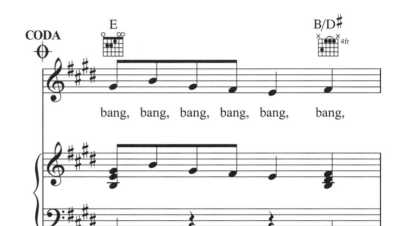

bang.   Bang, bang,   bang, bang, bang, bang, bang. Been a   hell of a ride, ___ but I'm

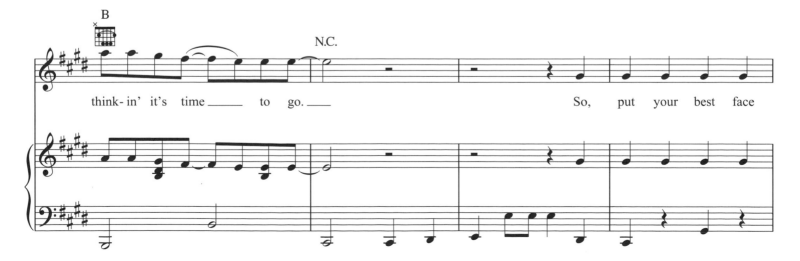

think-in' it's time _____ to go. ___   So, put your best face

on, ev-'ry-bod-y. Pre-tend you know this song, ev-'ry-bod-y. Come

hang. Let's go out___ with a bang. ___ Bang, bang,

bang! (Here we go.) So, put your best face on, ev-'ry-bod-y. Pre-

tend you know this song, ev-'ry-bod-y. Come hang,

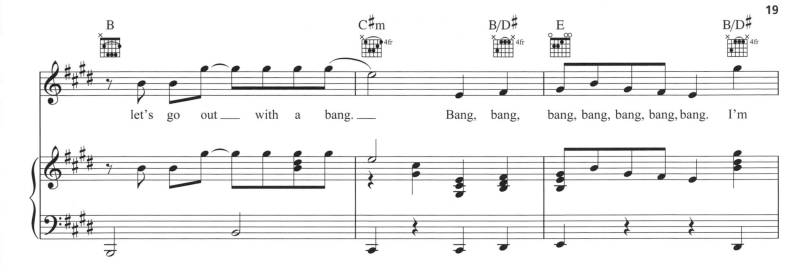

let's go out___ with a bang.___ Bang, bang, bang, bang, bang, bang, bang. I'm

way too young to lie here for - ev - er. I'm way too old to

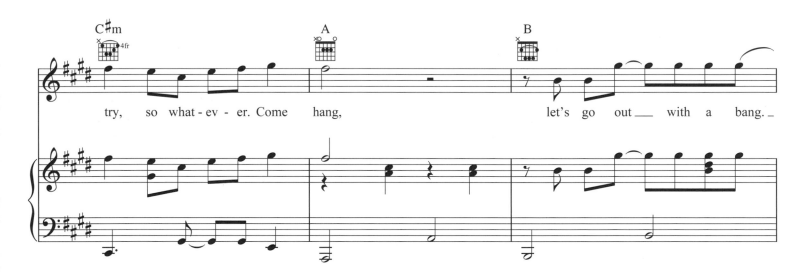

try, so what - ev - er. Come hang, let's go out___ with a bang.___

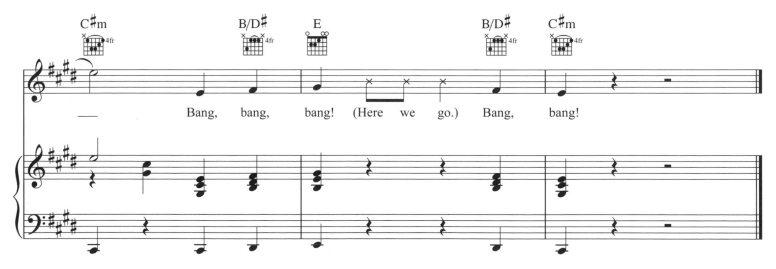

___ Bang, bang, bang! (Here we go.) Bang, bang!

DIAMONDS

Words and Music by SAM SMITH,
OSCAR GORRES and SHELLBACK

* *Recorded a half step higher.*

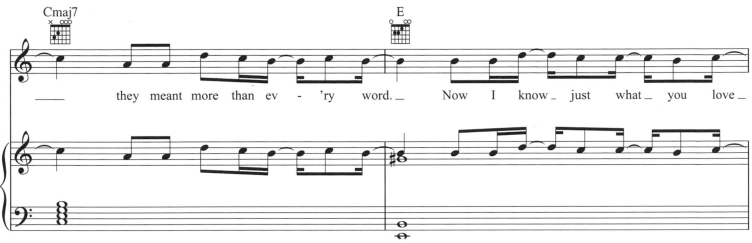

they meant more than ev - 'ry word. Now I know_ just what_ you love_

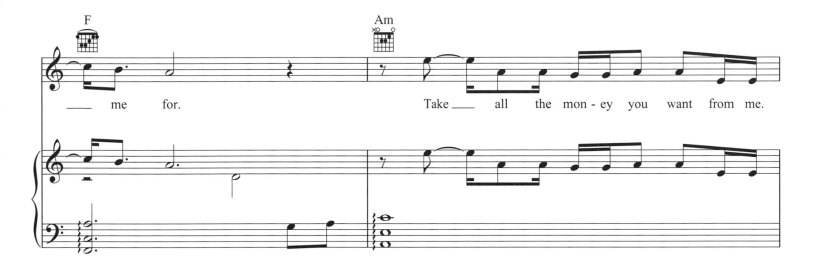

_ me for. Take _ all the mon - ey you want from me.

Hope _ you be - come what you want to be. Show _ me how lit - tle you care, how

lit - tle you care, how lit - tle you care. You _ dream of glit - ter and gold.

-i-ly.__ You lied _____ to me, __ lie, lied _____ to me, _____ then left __

__ with my __ heart 'round _ your chest. _____

Take __ all the mon-ey you want from me. Hope __ you be-come what you want to be.

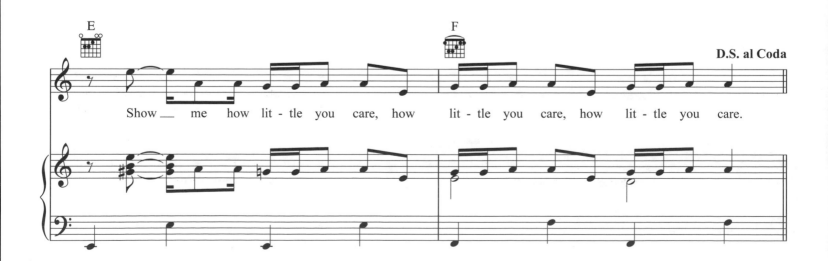

Show __ me how lit-tle you care, how lit-tle you care, how lit-tle you care.

fool me. ___ When you're not here I can breathe. ___ Think I al-ways knew my dia-monds leave with

you. You're nev-er gon-na hear my heart break, ___ nev-er gon-na move in

dark ways. ___ Ba-by, you're so cruel. My dia-monds leave with

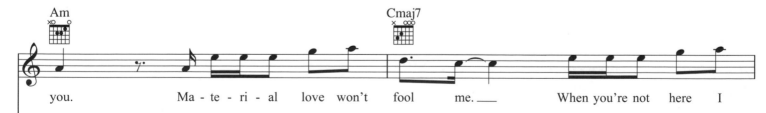

you. Ma-te-ri-al love won't fool me. ___ When you're not here I

DRIVERS LICENSE

Words and Music by DANIEL NIGRO
and OLIVIA RODRIGO

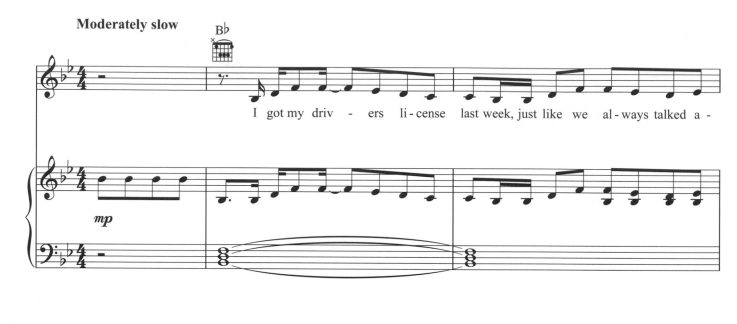

I got my driv - ers li - cense last week, just like we al - ways talked a -

bout. 'Cause you were so ex - cit - ed for me to fi - n'lly drive up to your

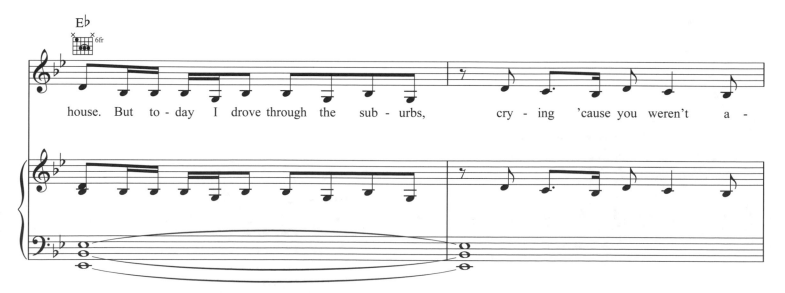

house. But to - day I drove through the sub - urbs, cry - ing 'cause you weren't a -

I know we weren't per-fect, but I've nev-er felt this way for no one. And

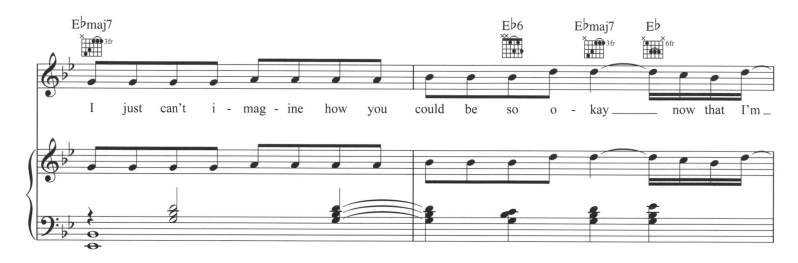

I just can't i-mag-ine how you could be so o-kay _____ now that I'm _____

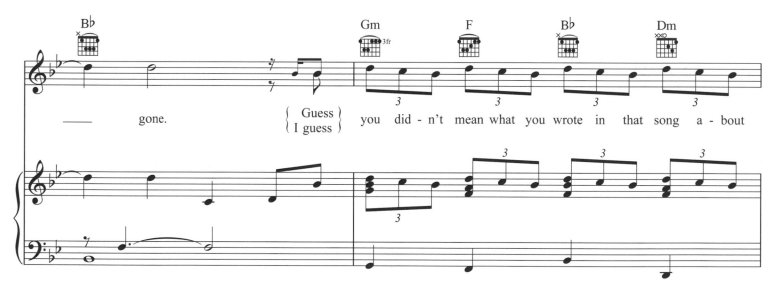

_____ gone. { Guess / I guess } you did-n't mean what you wrote in that song a-bout

me. _____ 'Cause you said for-ev-er; now I drive a-lone past your

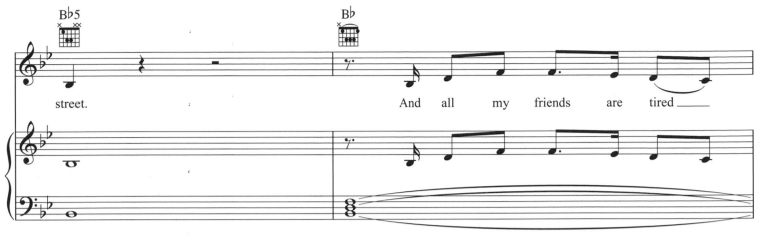

And all my friends are tired ____

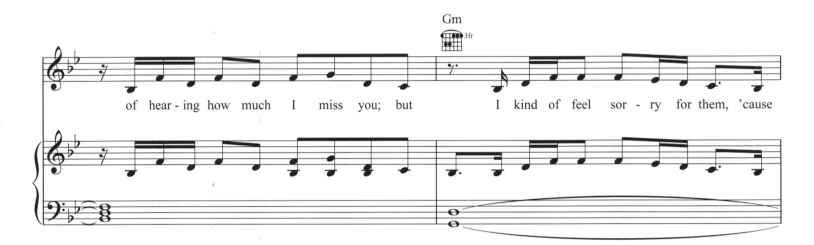

of hear - ing how much I miss you; but I kind of feel sor - ry for them, 'cause

they'll nev - er know you the way that I do. Yeah, to - day I drove through the sub - urbs ____ and

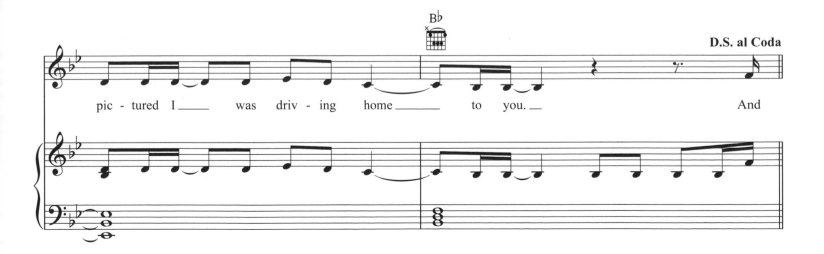

pic - tured I ____ was driv - ing home ____ to you. ____ And

D.S. al Coda

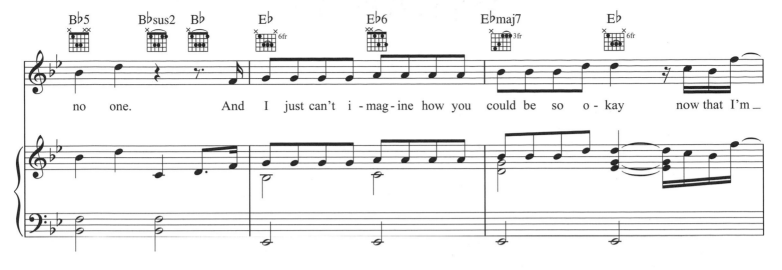

no one. And I just can't i-mag-ine how you could be so o-kay now that I'm _

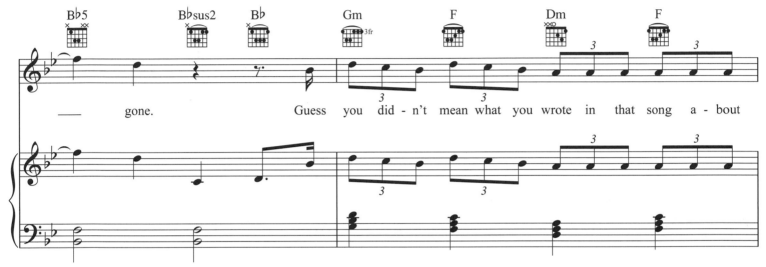

_ gone. Guess you did-n't mean what you wrote in that song a-bout

me. 'Cause you said for-ev-er; now I drive a-lone past your street. Yeah,

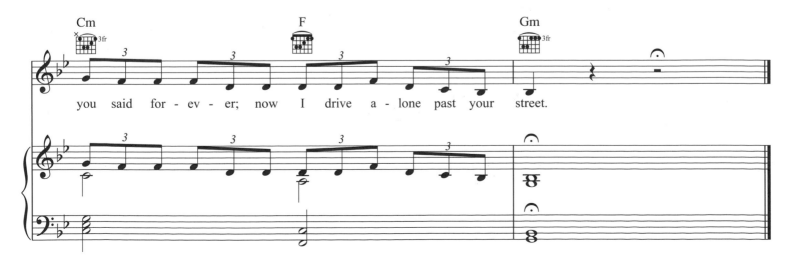

you said for-ev-er; now I drive a-lone past your street.

DYNAMITE

Words and Music by JESSICA AGOMBAR
and DAVID STEWART

Moderately fast

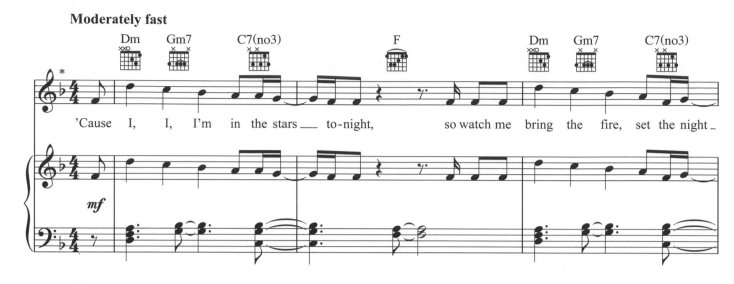

'Cause I, I, I'm in the stars __ to-night, so watch me bring the fire, set the night __

__ a-light. Show's on, I get up in the morn, cup of milk, let's rock and roll.

King Kong, kick the drum, __ roll-ing on like a Roll-ing Stone. Sing song when I'm walk-ing home, __ jump

* Recorded a half step lower.

up to the top, Le-Bron. Ding-dong, call me on my phone, iced tea and a game of Ping-Pong.

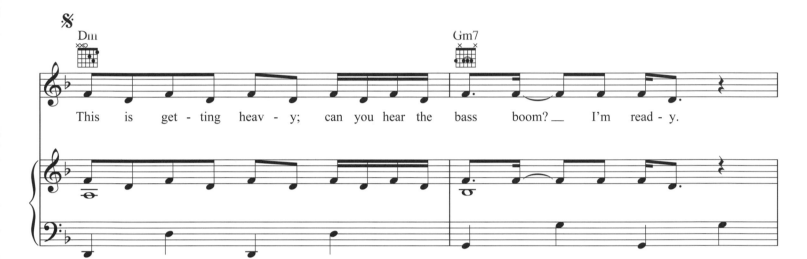

This is get-ting heav-y; can you hear the bass boom? __ I'm read-y.

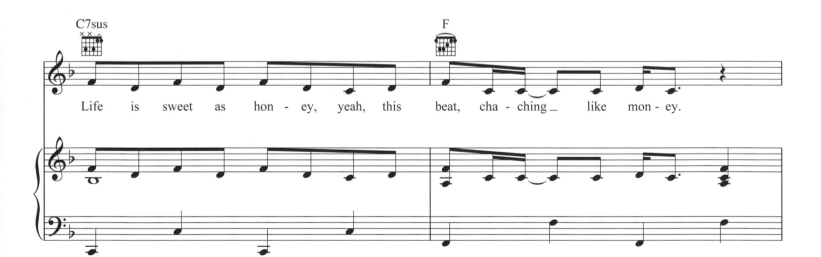

Life is sweet as hon-ey, yeah, this beat, cha-ching __ like mon-ey.

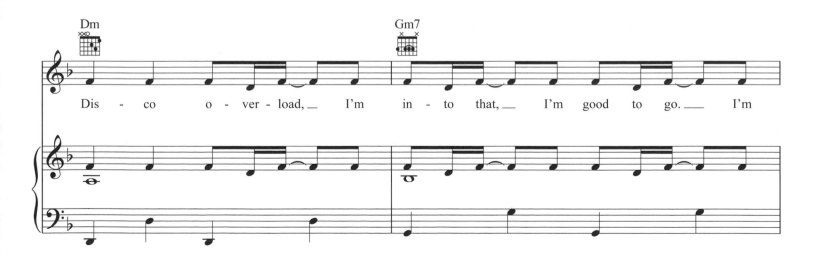

Dis - co o - ver-load, __ I'm in - to that, __ I'm good to go. __ I'm

dia - mond; __ you know I glow up. (Hey, so let's go!) / (Hey, let's go!) 'Cause I, I, I'm in the stars __

__ to - night, so watch me bring the fire, set the night __ a - light.

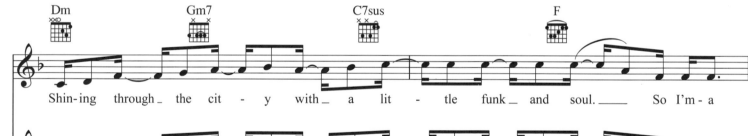

Shin - ing through __ the cit - y with __ a lit - tle funk __ and soul. __ So I'm - a

To Coda ⊕

light it up like dy - na - mite. Whoa. ___

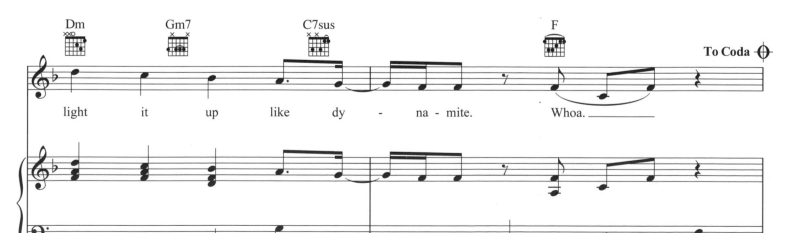

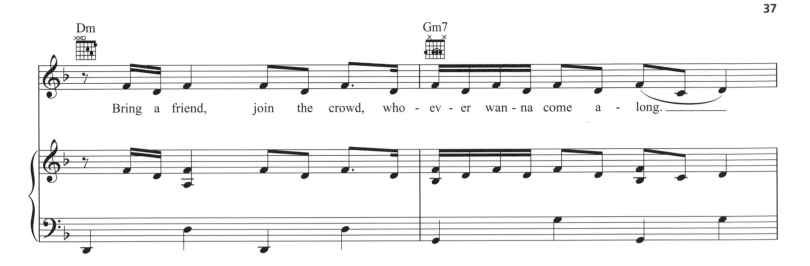

Bring a friend, join the crowd, who-ev-er wan-na come a-long. ___

Word up, talk the talk, ___ just move like we off the wall. ___

Day or night, the sky's a-light, ___ so we dance to the break of dawn.

D.S. al Coda

(La-dies and gen-tle-men, I got the med-i-cine, so you should keep your eyes on the ball.)

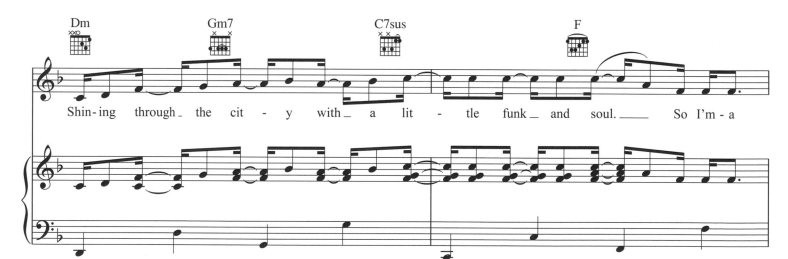

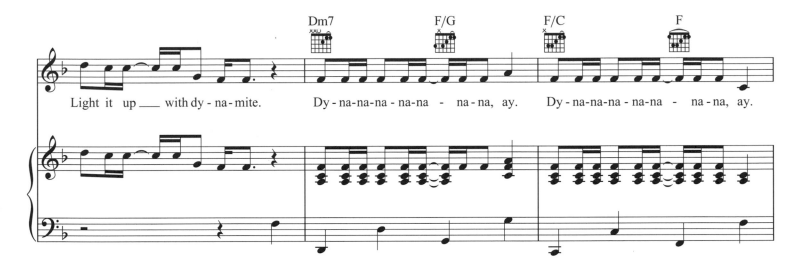

Dy - na - na - na - na - na - na - na, ay. Dy - na - na - na - na - na - na - na, ay.

Light it up ___ with dy - na - mite. Dy - na - na - na - na - na - na - na, ay. Dy - na - na - na - na - na - na - na, ay.

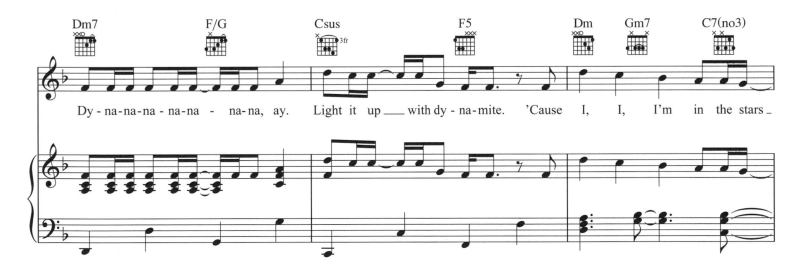

Dy - na - na - na - na - na - na - na, ay. Light it up ___ with dy - na - mite. 'Cause I, I, I'm in the stars ___

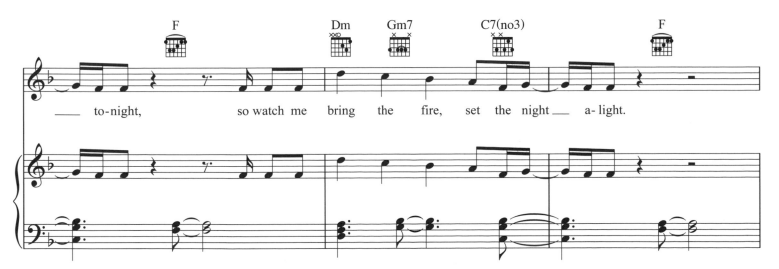

___ to - night, so watch me bring the fire, set the night ___ a - light.

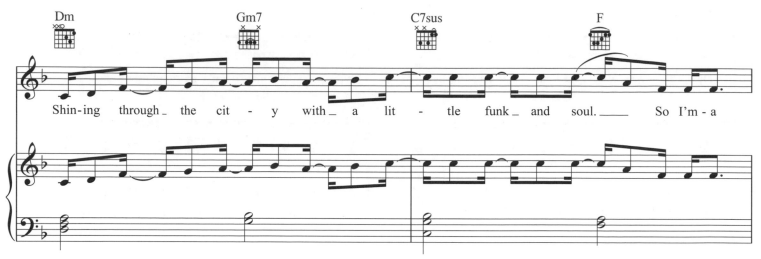

Shin-ing through the cit - y with a lit - tle funk and soul. So I'm a

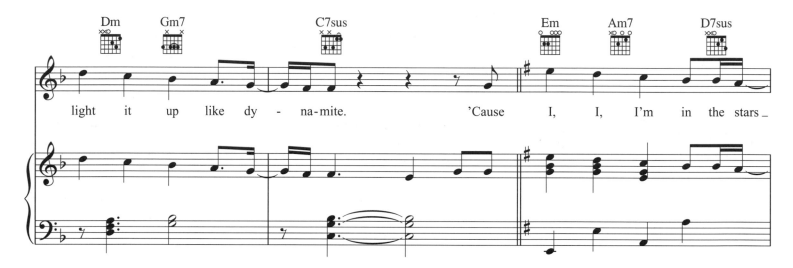

light it up like dy - na-mite. 'Cause I, I, I'm in the stars

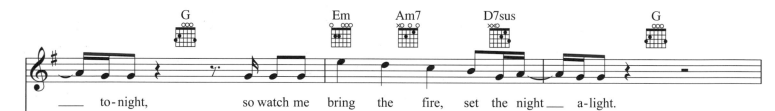

___ to-night, so watch me bring the fire, set the night ___ a-light.

Shin ing through the cit - y with a lit - tle funk and soul. So I'm a

light it up like dy - na-mite. Whoa. ___ Dy - na-na-na-na-na - na-na-na-na-na-

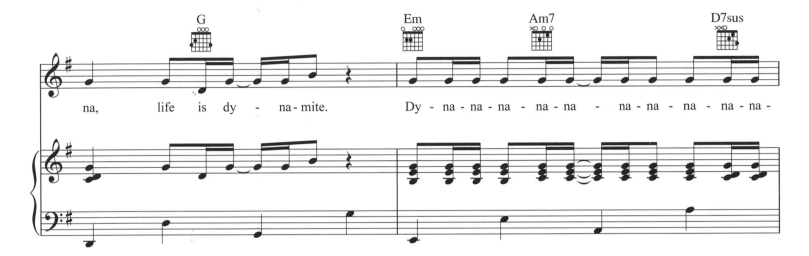

na, life is dy - na-mite. Dy - na-na-na-na-na - na-na-na-na-na-

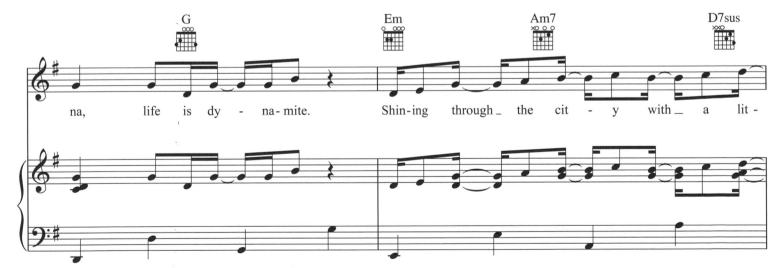

na, life is dy - na-mite. Shin-ing through_ the cit - y with_ a lit-

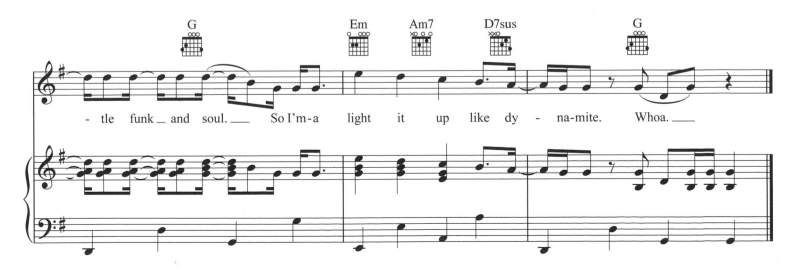

- tle funk_ and soul. ___ So I'm-a light it up like dy - na-mite. Whoa. ___

HAPPY ANYWHERE

Words and Music by ROSS COPPERMAN,
JOSH OSBORNE and MATT JENKINS

I've al-ways been a
Yeah, the beau-ty of the

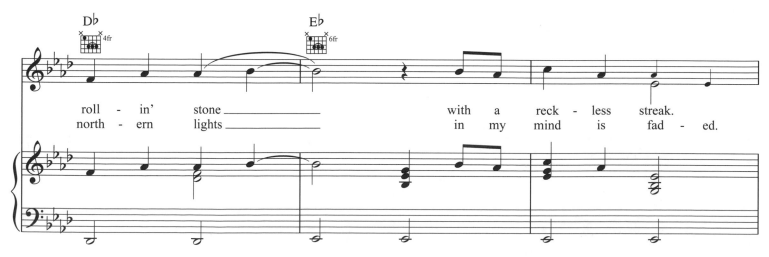

roll-in' stone _____ with a reck-less streak.
north-ern lights _____ in my mind is fad-ed.

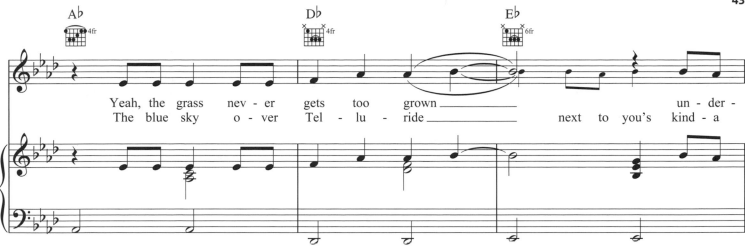

Yeah, the grass nev-er gets too grown _____ un-der-
The blue sky o-ver Tel-lu-ride _____ next to you's kind-a

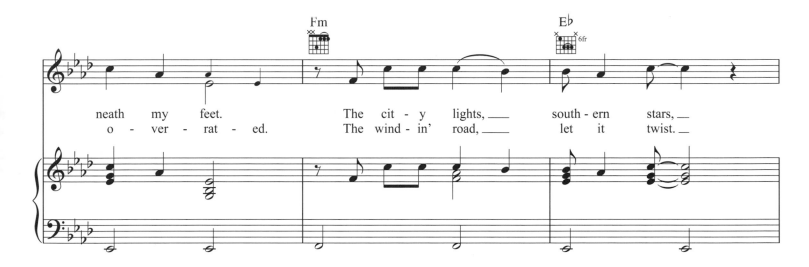

neath my feet. The cit-y lights, ___ south-ern stars, ___
o-ver-rat-ed. The wind-in' road, ___ let it twist. ___

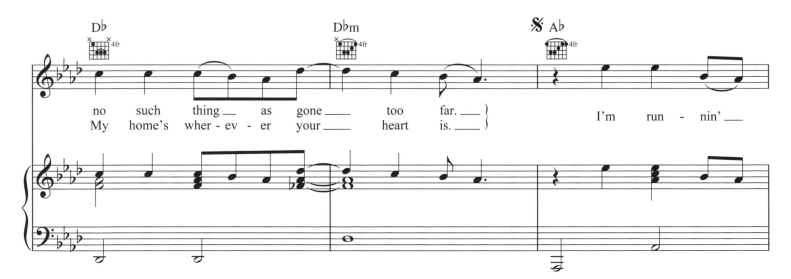

no such thing ___ as gone ___ too far. I'm run-nin' ___
My home's wher-ev-er your ___ heart is. ___

wide o-pen. ___ I was born with my feet in mo-tion. ___

But since I met you, ___ I swear I could be hap-py

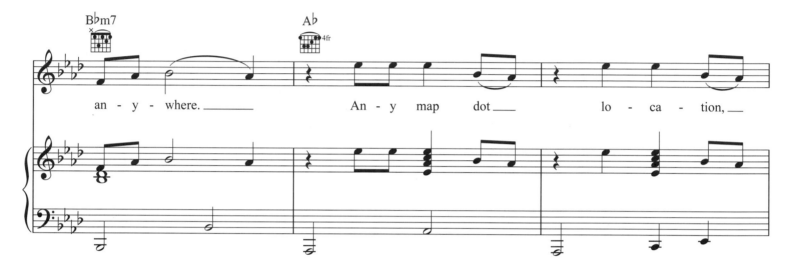

an - y - where. _____ An - y map dot ___ lo - ca - tion, ___

you're al - ways my des - ti - na - tion. ___ You're the on - ly thing that

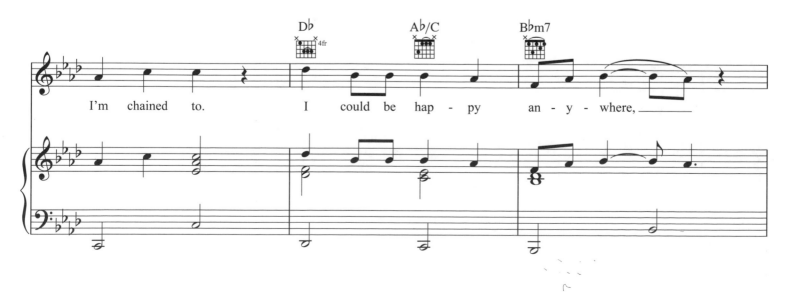

I'm chained to. I could be hap - py an - y - where, _____

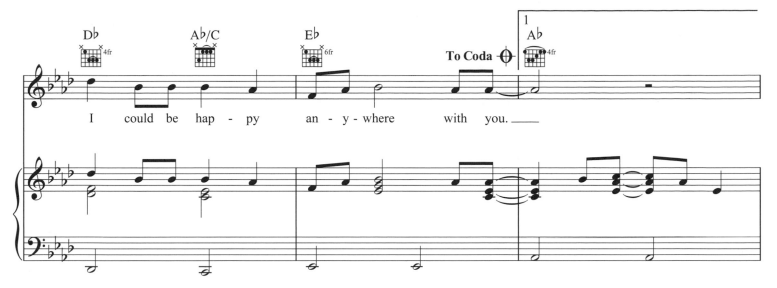

I could be hap - py an - y - where with you. ____

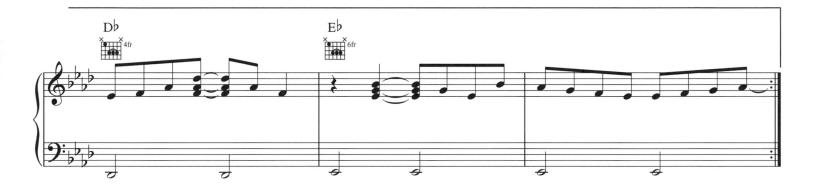

So, girl, ___ I hope you know ___ wher-ev-er you go, I go, I know. ___

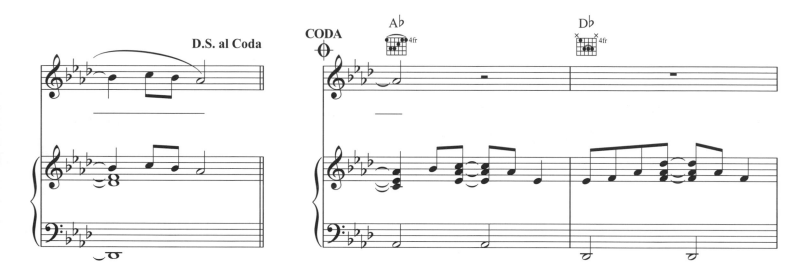

D.S. al Coda

CODA

I could be hap - py an-y-where ___ with you. ___

ICE CREAM

Words and Music by SELENA GOMEZ,
ARIANA GRANDE, TEDDY PARK,
JUNG HUN SEO, VICTORIA MONÉT McCANTS,
TOMMY BROWN, STEVEN FRANKS
and REBECCA JOHNSON

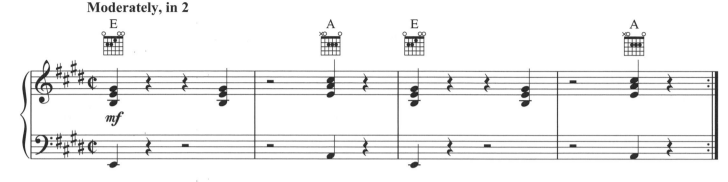

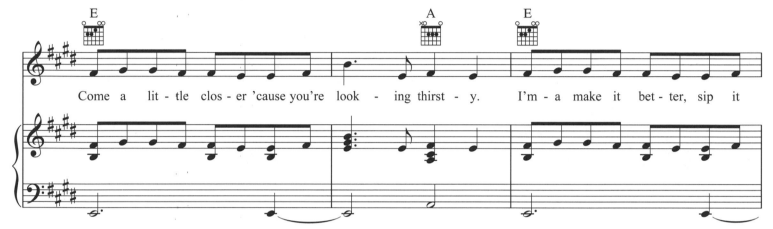

Come a lit-tle clos-er 'cause you're look-ing thirst-y. I'm-a make it bet-ter, sip it

like a Slur-pee. Snow cone chil-ly, get it free like Wil-ly. In the

jeans like Bil-lie, you be pop-ping like a wheel-ie. E-ven in the sun, you know I

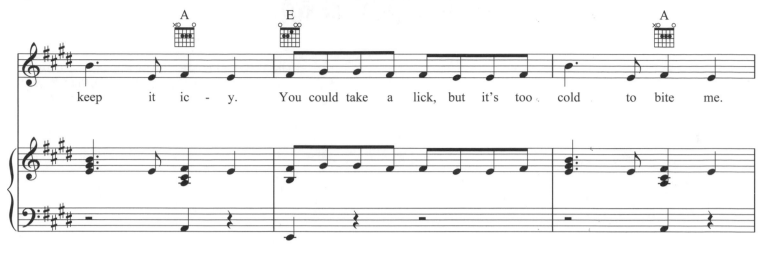

keep it ic - y. You could take a lick, but it's too cold to bite me.

Brr, brr, fro - zen, you're the one been cho - sen. Play the part like Mos - es, keep it

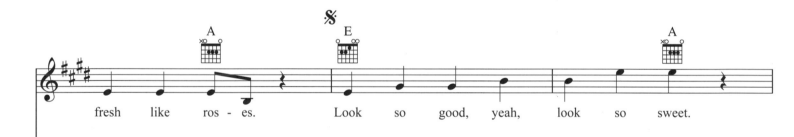

fresh like ros - es. Look so good, yeah, look so sweet.

Look - ing good e - nough to eat. Cold - est with the kiss, so he

49

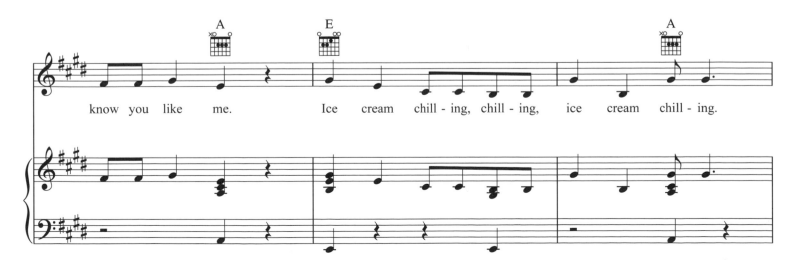

I can't see no-bod-y else for me, no. Get it, flip it, scoop it,

do it like that, oh yeah, oh yeah. Like it, love it, lick it, do it like la - la - la, oh yeah.

D.S. al Coda

CODA

ice cream, chill - ing. Ice cream chill - ing, chill - ing, ice cream chill - ing.

Ice cream chill - ing, chill - ing, ice cream. Chill - in' like a vil - lain, yeah,

N.C.

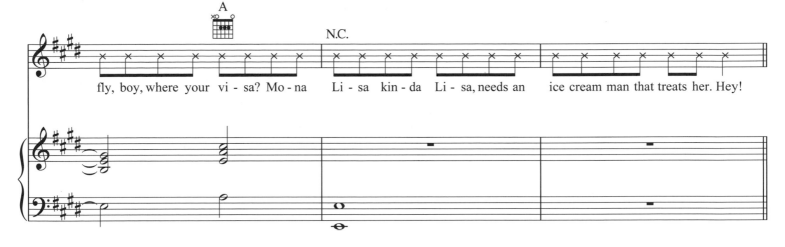

fly, boy, where your vi - sa? Mo - na Li - sa kin - da Li - sa, needs an ice cream man that treats her. Hey!

Na na na na na, na na na na na. Ice on my wrist, yeah, I

like it like this. { Get the bag } with the cream if you know what I mean.
{ And I'm nice }

1.
Ice cream, ice cream, ice cream chill - ing.

2.
Ice cream, ice cream, ice cream.

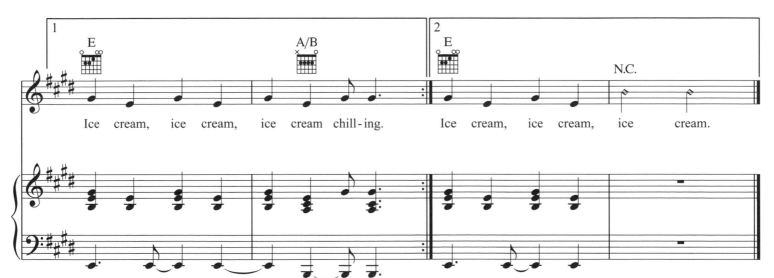

HOLY

Words and Music by JUSTIN BIEBER,
JON BELLION, ANTHONY JONES,
TOMMY BROWN, STEVEN FRANKS,
MICHAEL POLLACK, JORGEN ODEGARD
and CHANCELOR BENNETT

Recorded a half step lower.

'cause the way that the sky o-pens up when we touch, yeah, it's
but the way that we love in the night gave me life, ba - by.

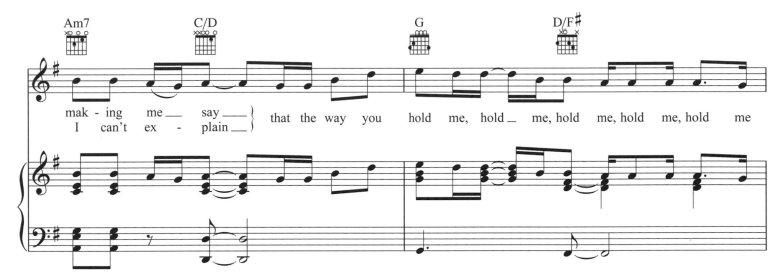

mak-ing me ___ say ___ that the way you hold me, hold ___ me, hold me, hold me, hold me
I can't ex - plain ___

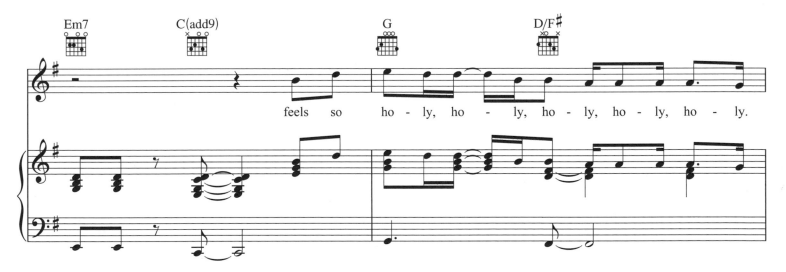

feels so ho - ly, ho - ly, ho - ly, ho - ly, ho - ly.

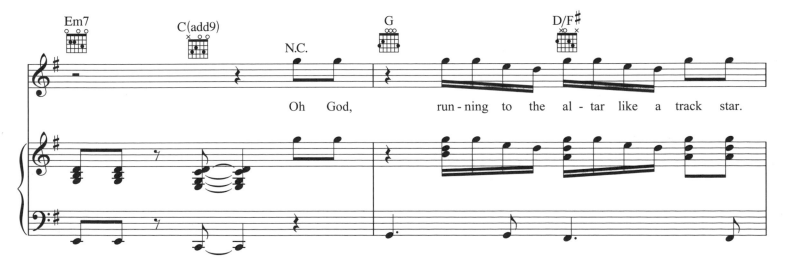

Oh God, run - ning to the al - tar like a track star.

Can't wait an-oth-er sec-ond 'cause the way you hold me, hold me, hold me, hold me, hold me

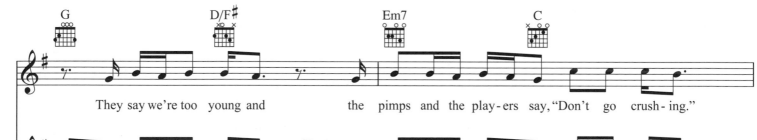

1
feels so _____ ho - ly.

2
feels so _____ ho - ly.

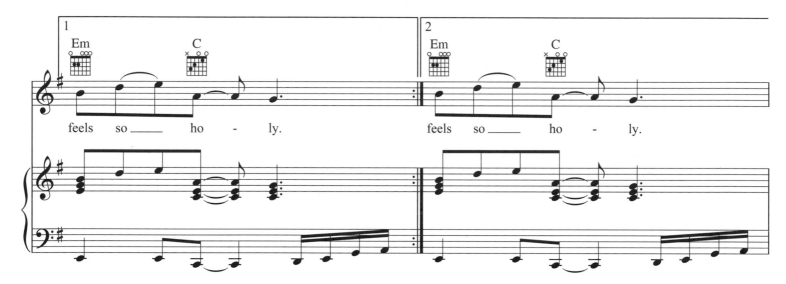

They say we're too young and the pimps and the play-ers say, "Don't go crush-ing."

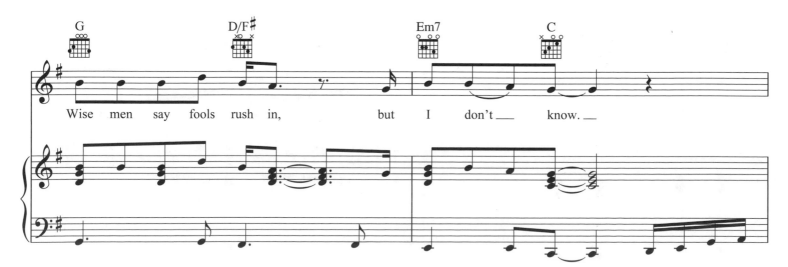

Wise men say fools rush in, but I don't _____ know. __

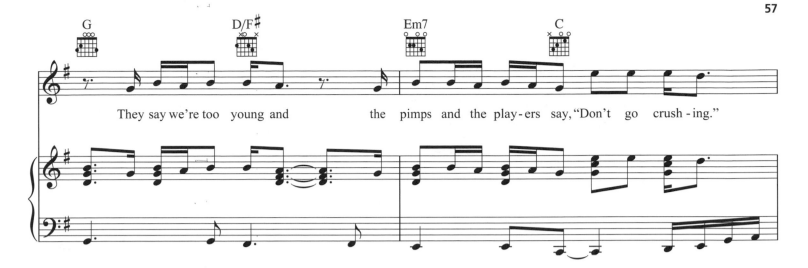

They say we're too young and the pimps and the play-ers say, "Don't go crush-ing."

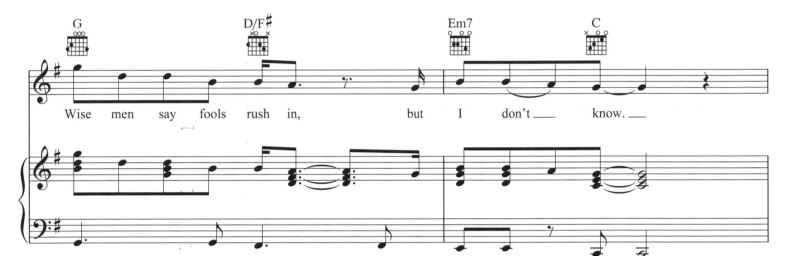

Wise men say fools rush in, but I don't ___ know. ___

The first step pleas-es the Fa - ther.

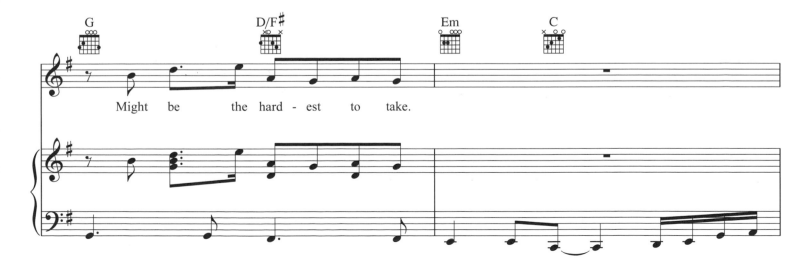

Might be the hard-est to take.

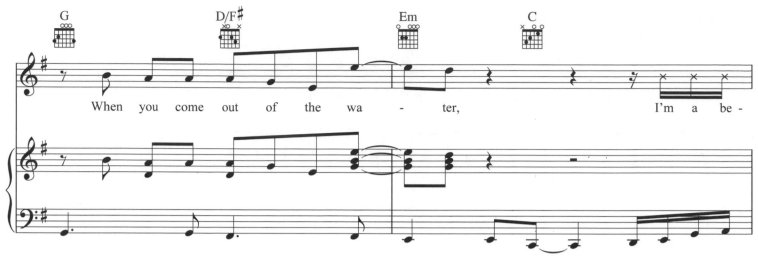

When you come out of the wa - ter, I'm a be -

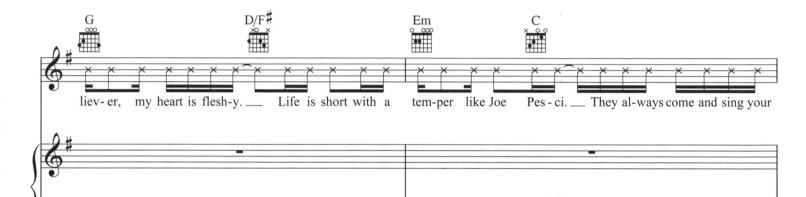

liev - er, my heart is flesh-y. __ Life is short with a tem-per like Joe Pes - ci. __ They al-ways come and sing your

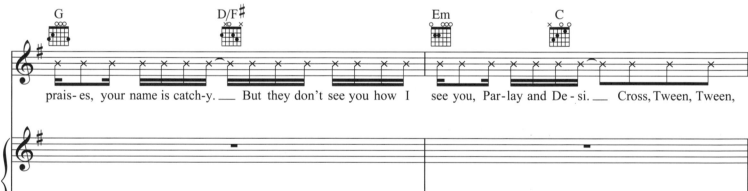

prais - es, your name is catch-y. __ But they don't see you how I see you, Par-lay and De - si. __ Cross, Tween, Tween,

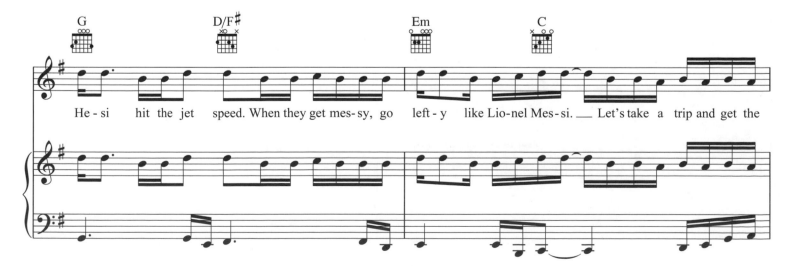

He - si hit the jet speed. When they get mes-sy, go left - y like Lio-nel Mes-si. __ Let's take a trip and get the

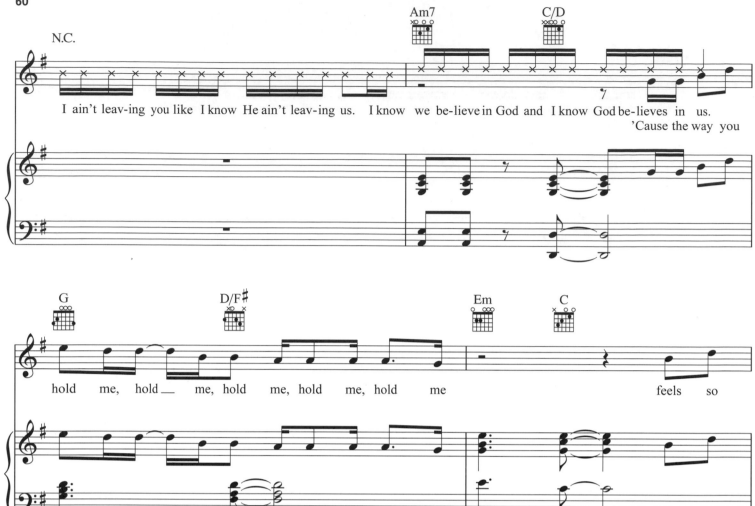

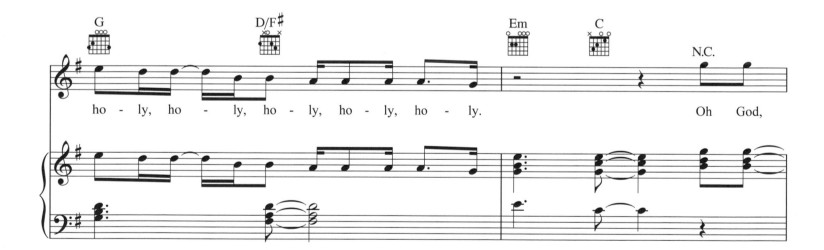

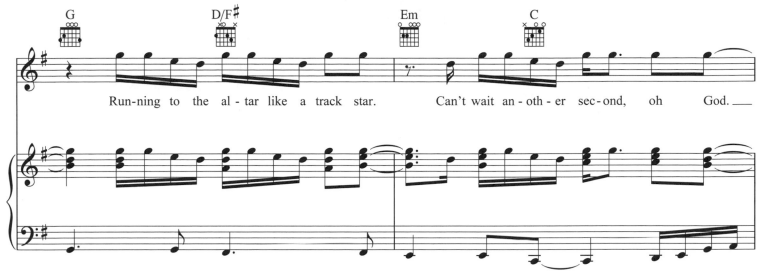

Run-ning to the al - tar like a track star. Can't wait an - oth - er sec-ond, oh God. ___

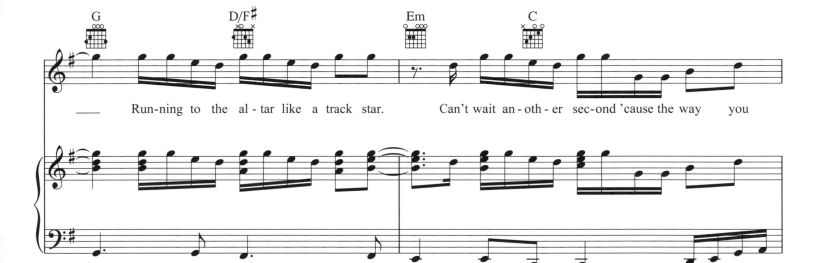

___ Run-ning to the al - tar like a track star. Can't wait an - oth - er sec-ond 'cause the way you

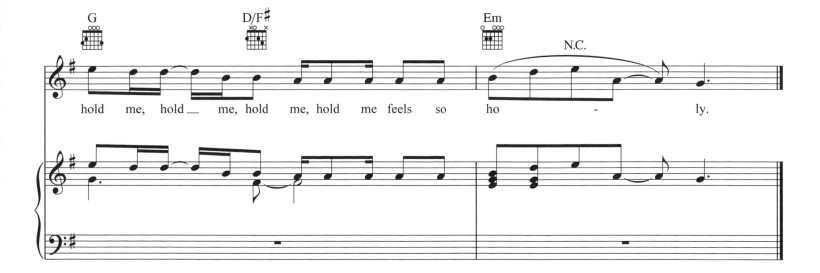

hold me, hold ___ me, hold me, hold me feels so ho - ly.

I HOPE

Words and Music by GABBY BARRETT,
ZACHARY KALE and JON NITE

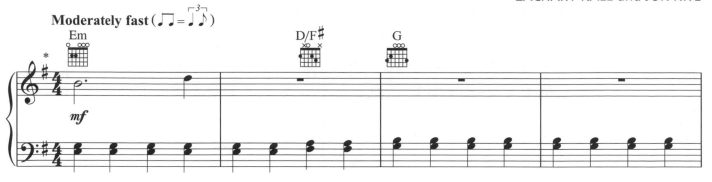

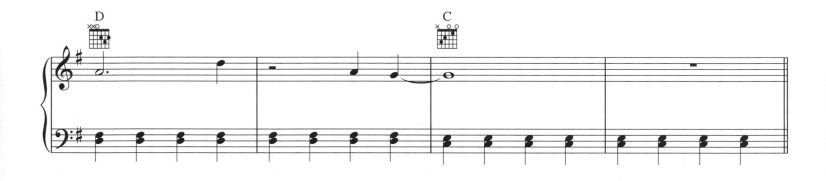

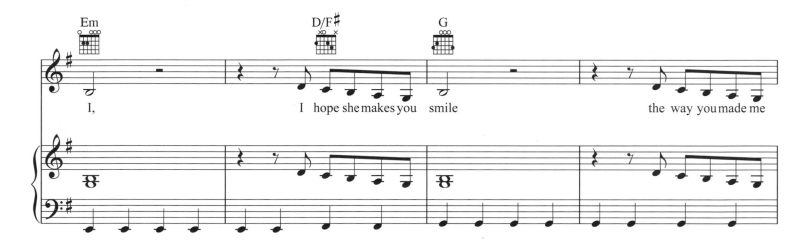

* *Recorded a half step lower.*

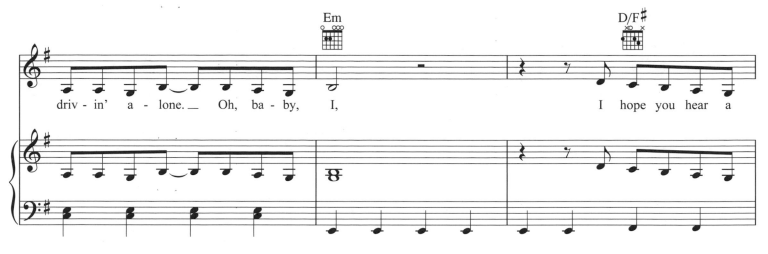

driv - in' a - lone. ___ Oh, ba - by, I, I hope you hear a

song that makes you sing a - long and gets you

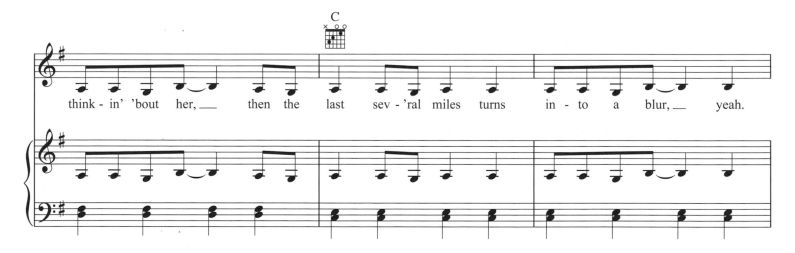

think - in' 'bout her, ___ then the last sev - 'ral miles turns in - to a blur, ___ yeah.

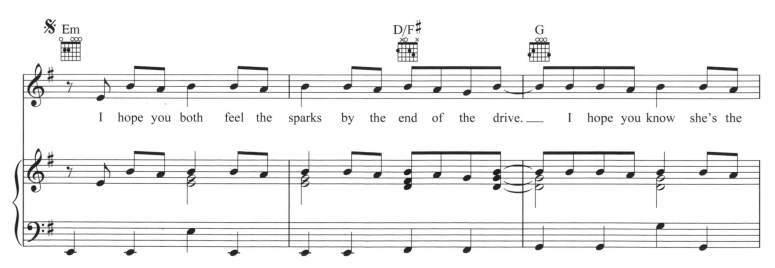

I hope you both feel the sparks by the end of the drive. ___ I hope you know she's the

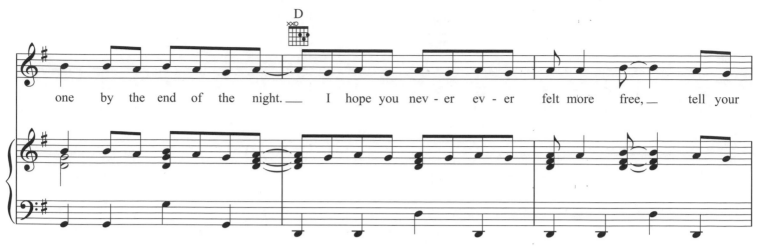

one by the end of the night. __ I hope you nev-er ev-er felt more free, __ tell your

friends that you're so hap - py. _____ I hope she comes a-long and

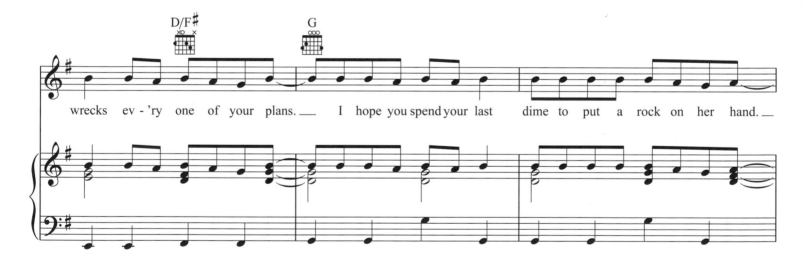

wrecks ev-'ry one of your plans. __ I hope you spend your last dime to put a rock on her hand. __

__ I hope she's wild-er than your wild-est dreams, __ she's ev-'ry-thing you're ev-er gon-na

need. And then I hope she cheats _____ like you did on

me. _____ And then I hope she cheats

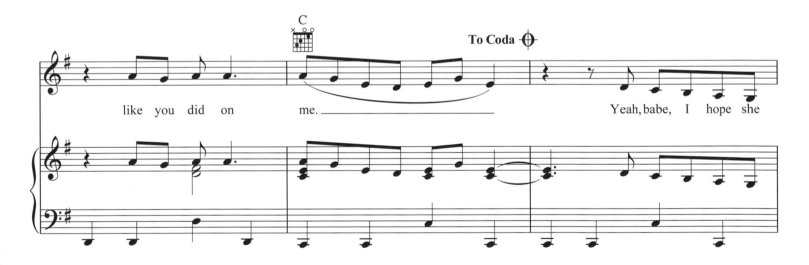

like you did on me. _____ Yeah, babe, I hope she

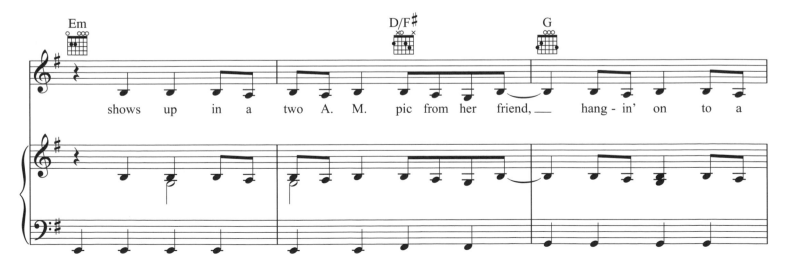

shows up in a two A. M. pic from her friend, ___ hang-in' on to a

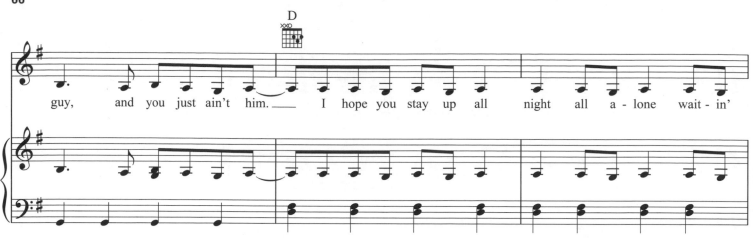

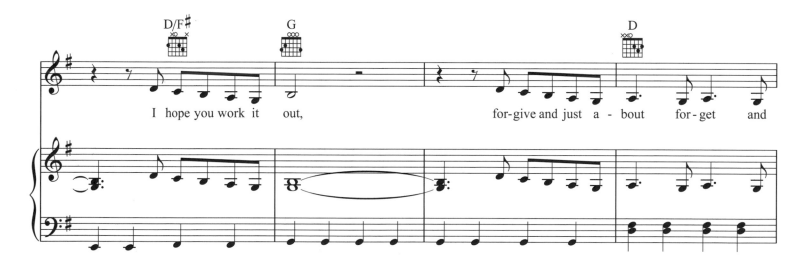

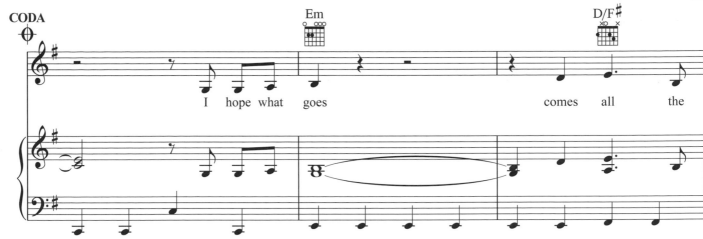

I hope what goes comes all the

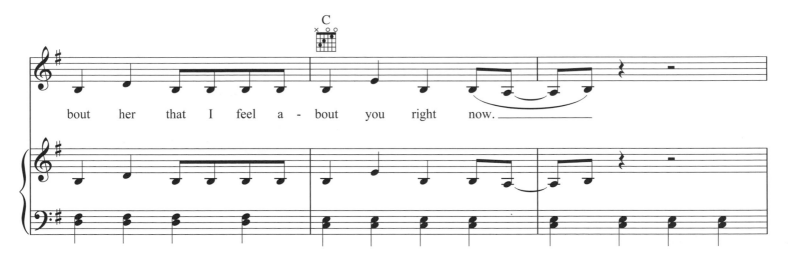

way a-round._____ I hope she makes you feel the same way a-

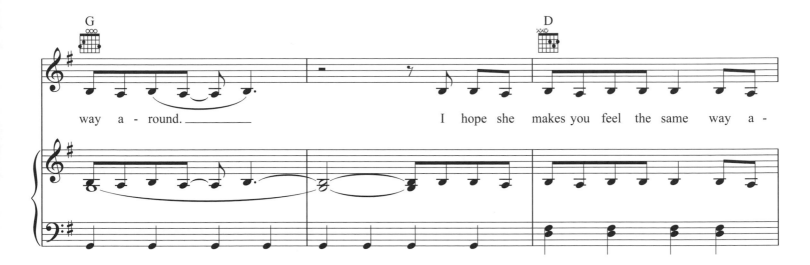

bout her that I feel a-bout you right now._____

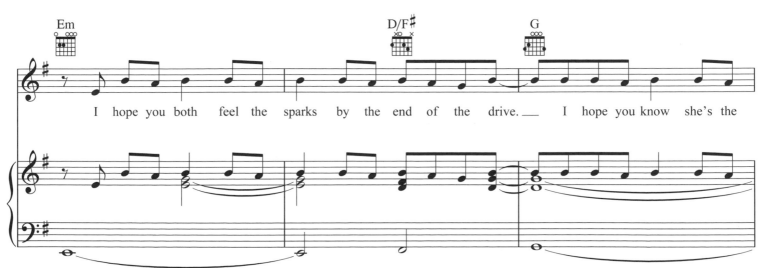

I hope you both feel the sparks by the end of the drive.__ I hope you know she's the

one by the end of the night.___ I hope you nev-er ev-er felt more free,___ tell your

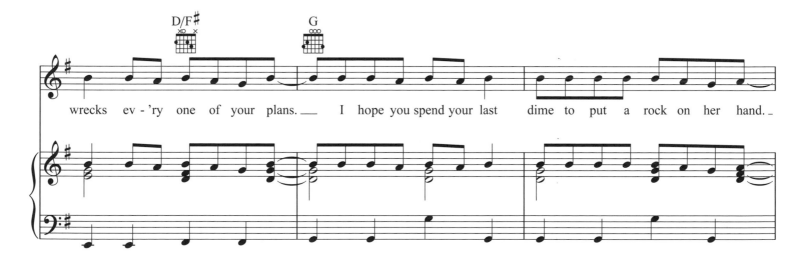

friends that you're so hap - py._____ I hope she comes a-long and

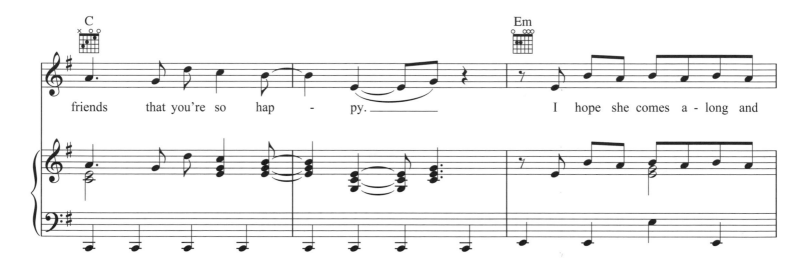

wrecks ev-'ry one of your plans.___ I hope you spend your last dime to put a rock on her hand.___

___ I hope she's wild-er than your wild-est dreams,___ she's ev-'ry-thing you're ev-er gon-na

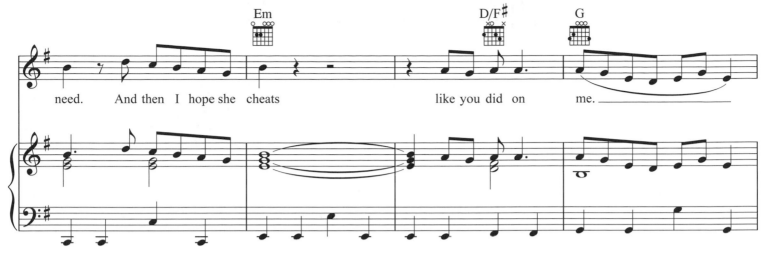

need. And then I hope she cheats like you did on me. ___

And then I hope she cheats like you did on me, ___

like you did on ___ me. ___

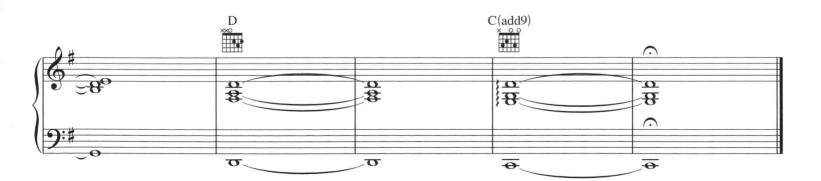

KINGS & QUEENS

Words and Music by DESMOND CHILD,
AMANDA KOCI, BRETT McLAUGHLIN,
HENRY WALTER, MADISON LOVE,
JAKOB ERIXSON, MIMOZA BLINSON,
NADIR KHAYAT and HILLARY BERNSTEIN

If all of the kings had their queens on the throne, we would pop champagne and raise a toast. To all of the queens who are fighting alone, baby, you're not dancing on your own. Can't live without me; you wanna, but you

can't, no no no. Think it's fun-ny, but hon-ey, can't run this show on your own. ____

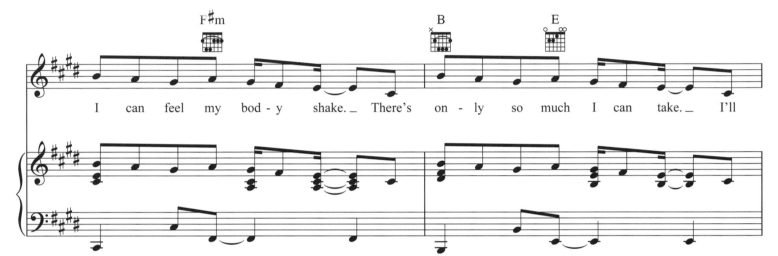

I can feel my bod-y shake. __ There's on-ly so much I can take. __ I'll

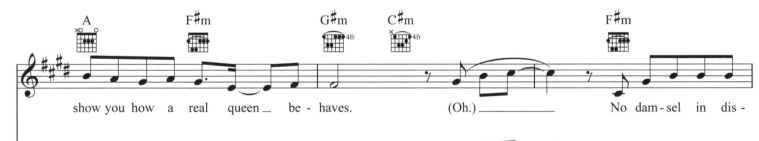

show you how a real queen __ be-haves. (Oh.) _____ No dam-sel in dis-

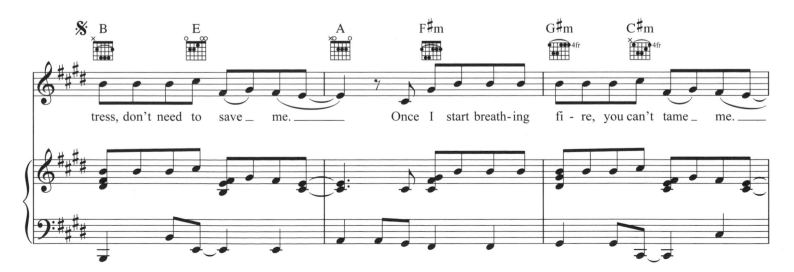

tress, don't need to save __ me. _____ Once I start breath-ing fi-re, you can't tame __ me. ____

on your own. Dis - o - bey me, then ba - by, it's off with your head. Gon - na

change it and make it a world you won't for - get. (Oh.) No dam - sel in dis -

D.S. al Coda

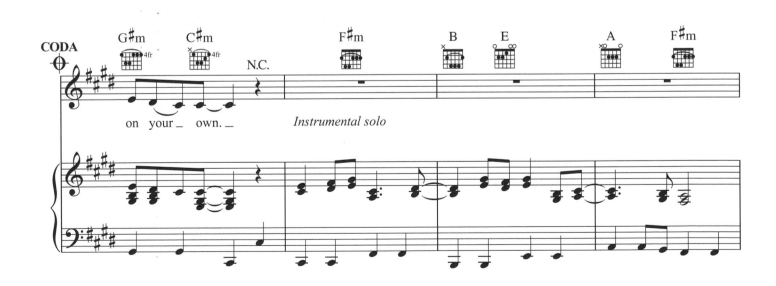

CODA

on your own. *Instrumental solo*

N.C.

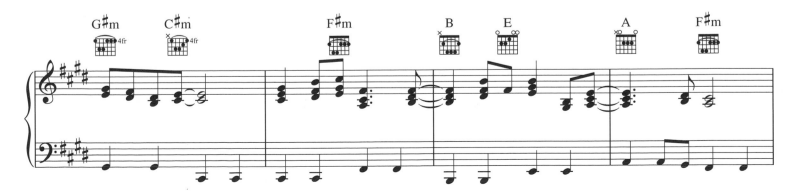

Solo ends In chess, the king can move one space at a time, __

but queens are free to go wher-ev-er they __ like. _____ You get too close, you'll get a

roy-al-ty high, __ so breathe it in to feel the love. _____

(If all of the kings __ had their queens on the throne, we would

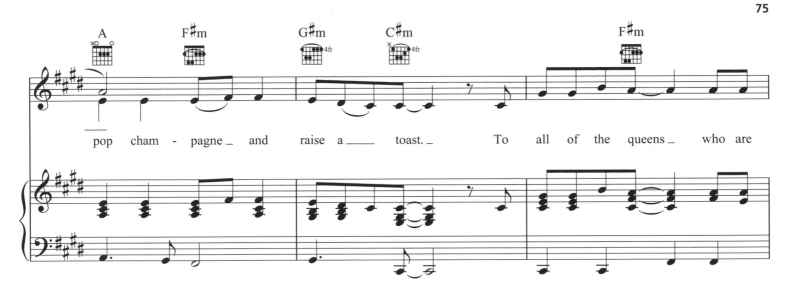

pop cham - pagne _ and raise a _ toast. _ To all of the queens _ who are

fight - ing a - lone, _ ba - by, you're not danc - ing on your _ own. _

Oh, _____ oh, _ oh, _____ oh.

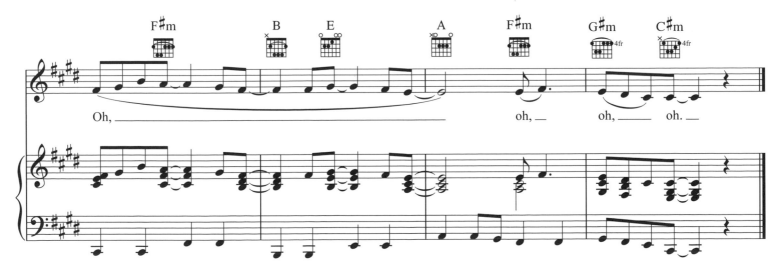

Oh, _____ oh, _ oh, _____ oh. _

MONSTER

Words and Music by JUSTIN BIEBER,
SHAWN MENDES, MUSTAFA AHMED,
ADAM FEENEY and ASHTON SIMMONDS

Half-time Pop

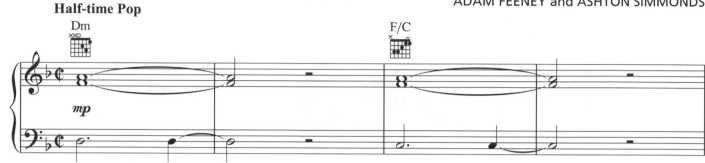

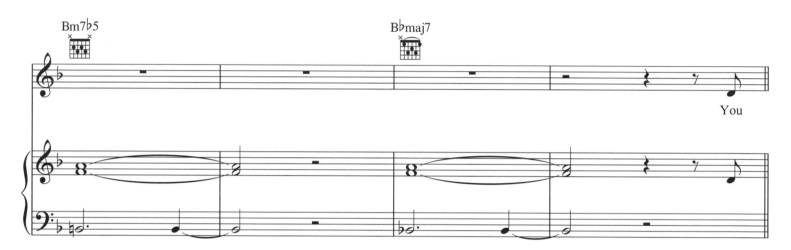

You

put me on a ped-es-tal and tell me I'm the best. ___

Raise me up in-to the sky un-til I'm short of breath. ___

Fill me up with con - fi - dence, I say what's in my chest. __ Spill my words and tear me down un -

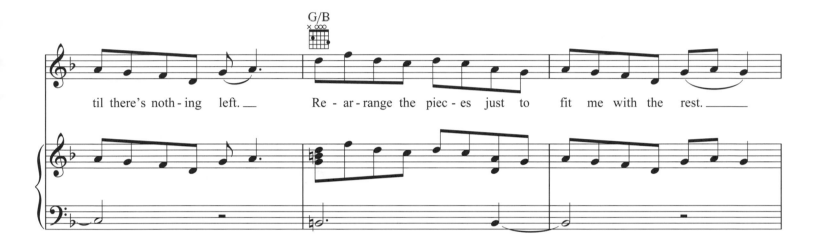

til there's noth - ing left. __ Re - ar - range the piec - es just to fit me with the rest. _____

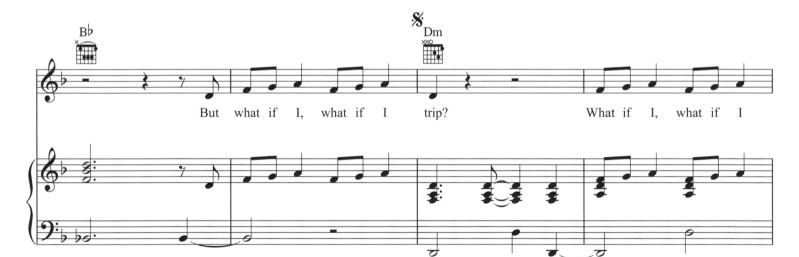

But what if I, what if I trip? What if I, what if I

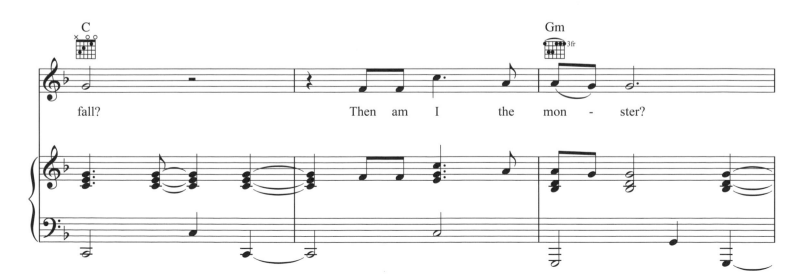

fall? Then am I the mon - ster?

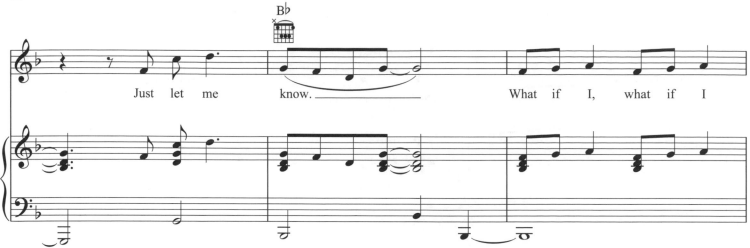

Just let me know. _____ What if I, what if I

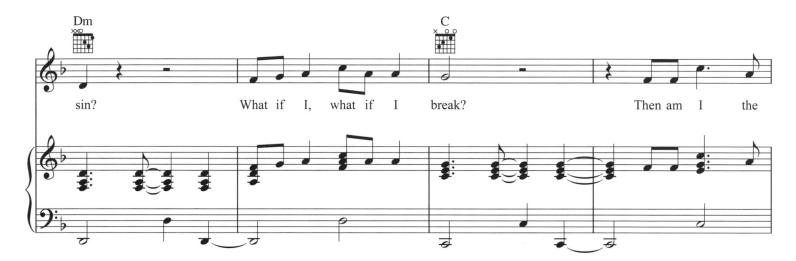

sin? What if I, what if I break? Then am I the

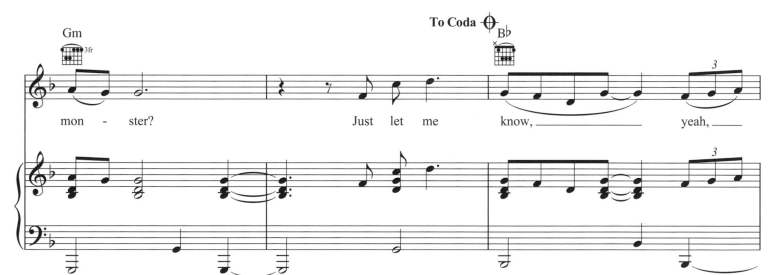

mon - ster? Just let me know, _____ yeah, _____

yeah, _ yeah, _ yeah. I was fif - teen when the world put me on a ped - es - tal. I had

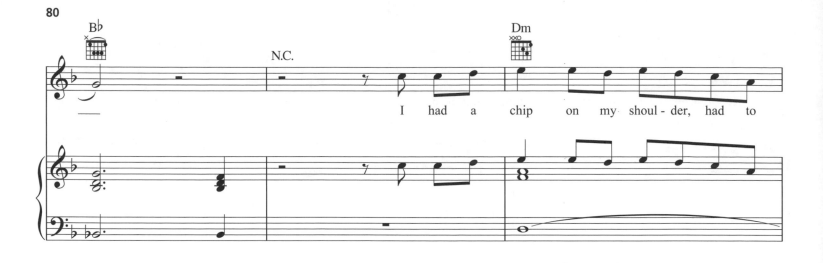

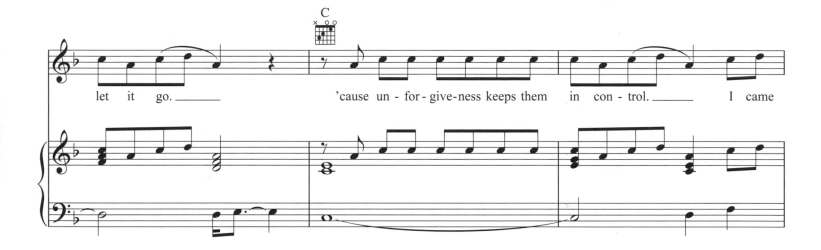

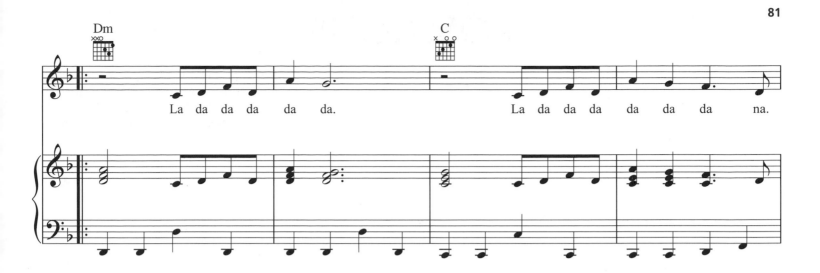

La da da da da da. La da da da da da da na.

La da da da da da. La da da da da da da na.

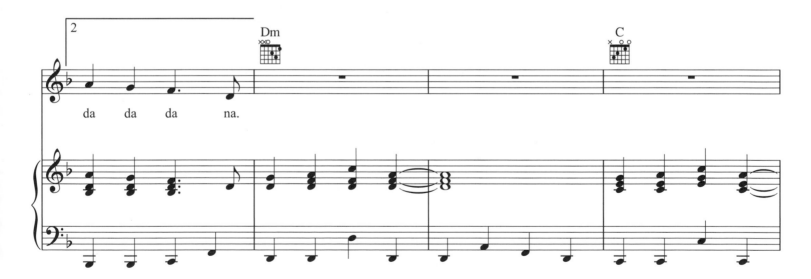

da da da na.

POSITIONS

Words and Music by ARIANA GRANDE,
NIJA CHARLES, TOMMY BROWN,
STEVEN FRANKS, ANGELINA BARRETT,
BRIAN BATES and LONDON HOLMES

Heav - en ___ sent you ___ to me.

I'm just ___ hop - ing ___ I don't re... ___

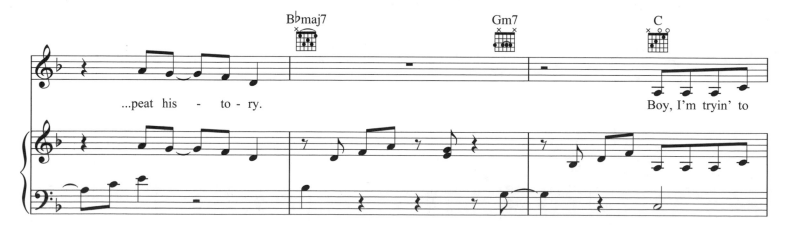

...peat his - to - ry.

Boy, I'm tryin' to

meet your ma - ma on a Sun - day, then make a lot __ of love on a Mon-

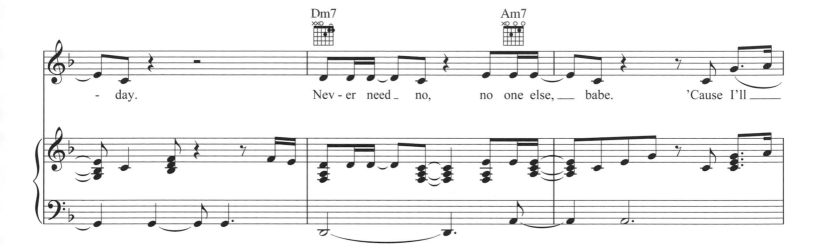

- day. Nev - er need __ no, no one else, __ babe. 'Cause I'll __

__ be __ switch-ing the po - si - tions for __ you. Cook-ing in the

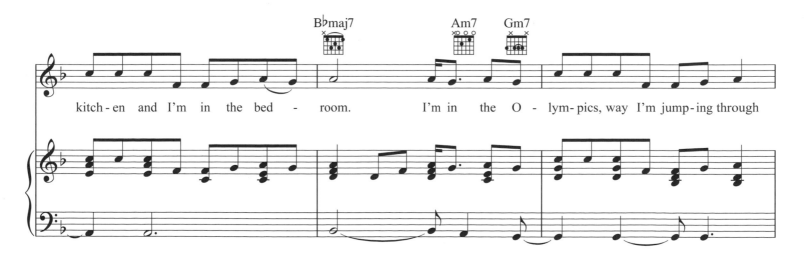

kitch - en and I'm in the bed - room. I'm in the O - lym - pics, way I'm jump-ing through

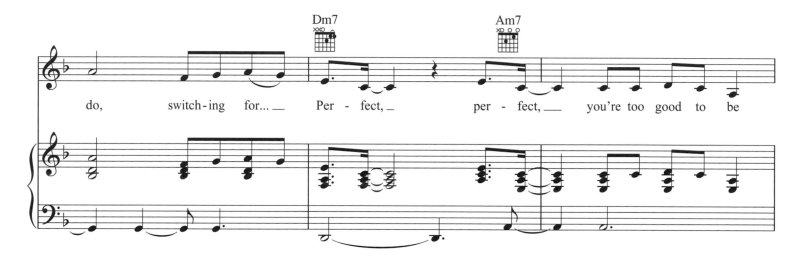

and I'm down, too. _____ Yeah, I'm down, too. Switch-ing the po - si - tions for _____

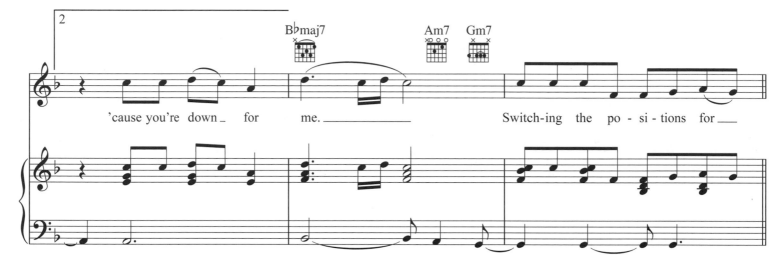

'cause you're down _ for me. _____ Switch-ing the po - si - tions for _____

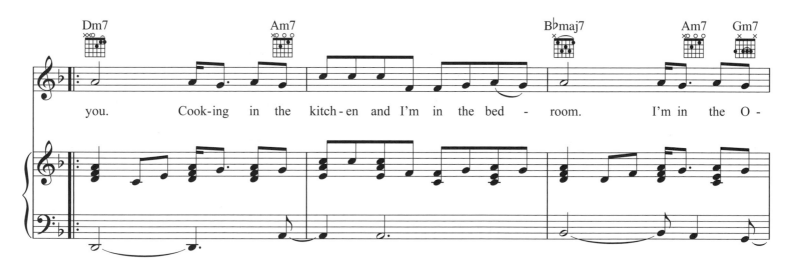

you. Cook-ing in the kitch-en and I'm in the bed - room. I'm in the O -

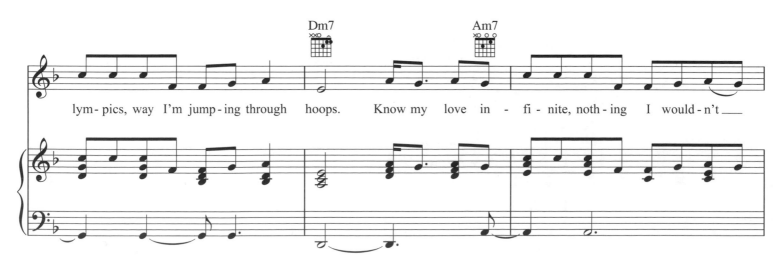

lym-pics, way I'm jump-ing through hoops. Know my love in - fi - nite, noth-ing I would-n't _____

do, that I won't _ do, switch-ing for ___ do, switch-ing for ___

you. _____ Yeah. _ Mm, ah, _____

yeah. Ah, _____ yeah. _

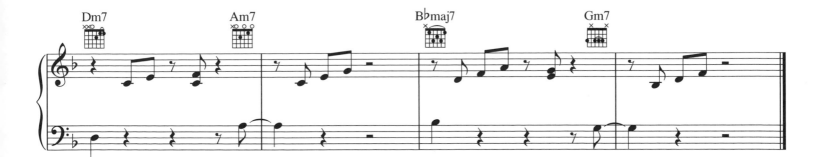

PRISONER

Words and Music by MILEY CYRUS,
DUA LIPA, JON BELLION,
JORDAN JOHNSON, MARCUS LOMAX,
ANDREW WATT, STEFAN JOHNSON,
ALI TAMPOSI and MICHAEL POLLACK

With energy

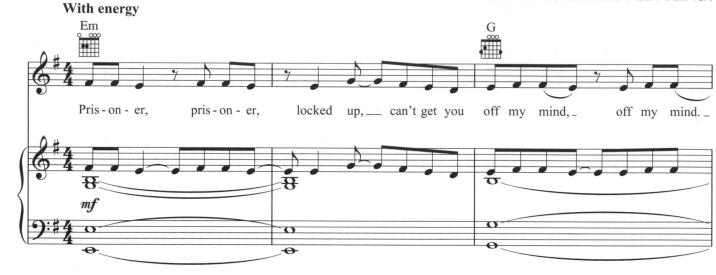

Pris-on-er, pris-on-er, locked up,___ can't get you off my mind,___ off my mind.

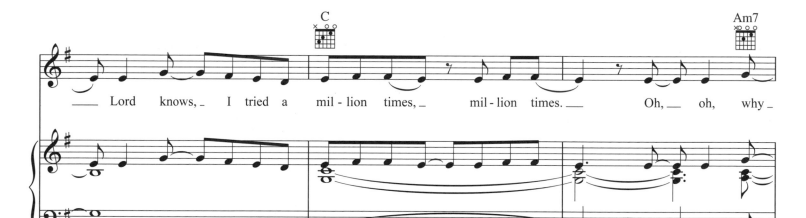

___ Lord knows,___ I tried a mil-lion times,___ mil-lion times.___ Oh,___ oh, why___

___ can't___ you, why can't___ you just let me go?

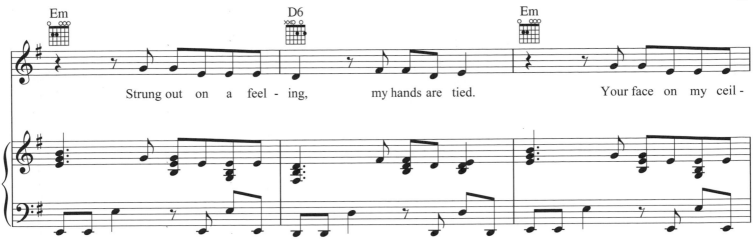

Strung out on a feel- ing, my hands are tied. Your face on my ceil-

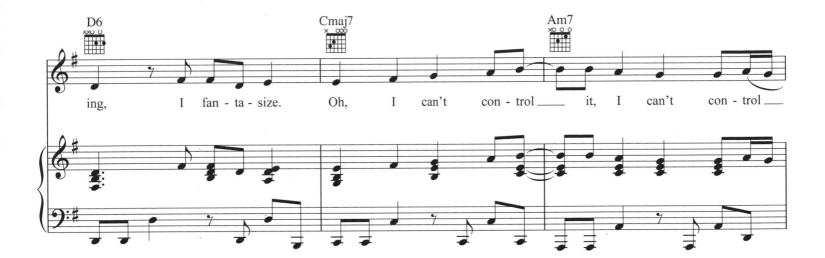

ing, I fan- ta- size. Oh, I can't con- trol___ it, I can't con- trol___

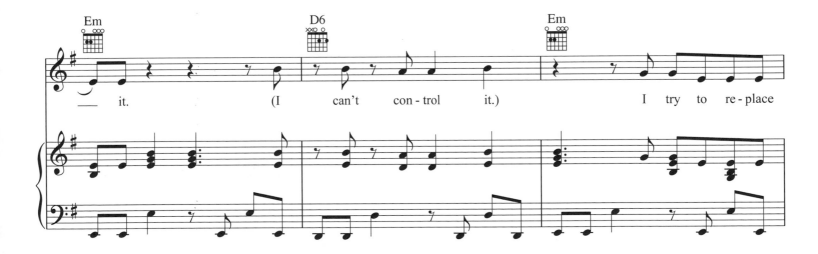

___ it. (I can't con- trol it.) I try to re- place

it with cit- y lights. I'll nev- er es- cape it, I need the high.

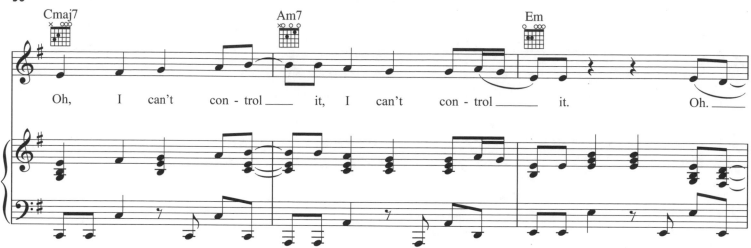

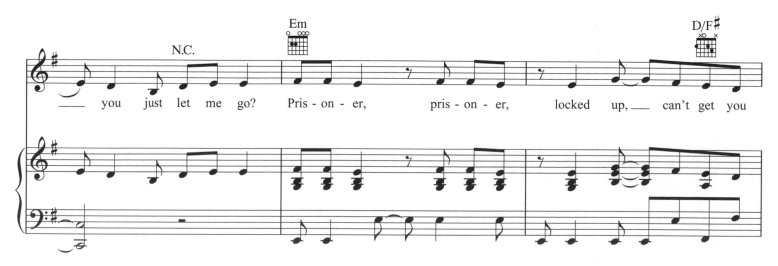

off my mind, __ off my mind. __ Lord knows, __ I tried a mil-lion times, __ mil-lion times. __

__ Oh, __ oh, why __ can't __ you, why can't __ you just let me go?

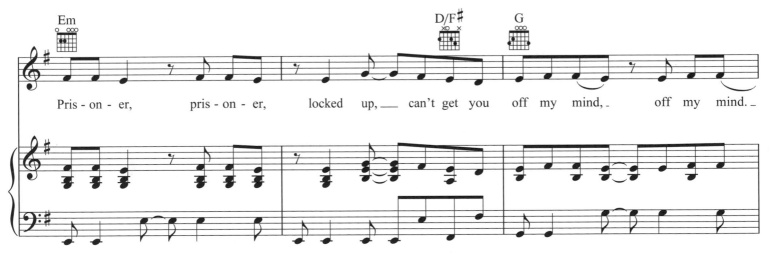

Pris-on-er, pris-on-er, locked up, __ can't get you off my mind, __ off my mind. __

__ Lord knows, __ I tried a mil-lion times, __ mil-lion times. __ Oh, __ oh, why __

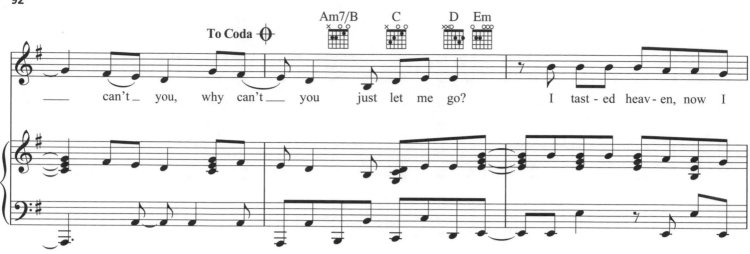

can't_ you, why can't__ you just let me go? I tast-ed heav-en, now I

can't live with-out__ it. I can't for-get you and your love is the loud - est.

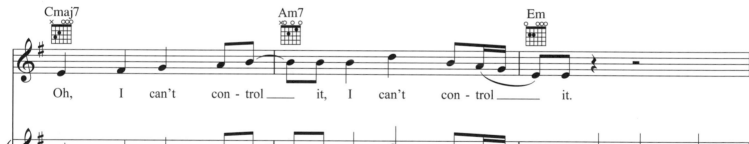

Oh, I can't con - trol___ it, I can't con - trol____ it.

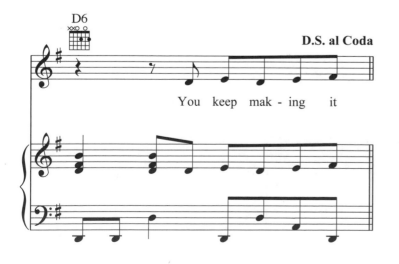

You keep mak-ing it

__ you just let me go?

Can't _ get you off my mind. _____ Why can't _

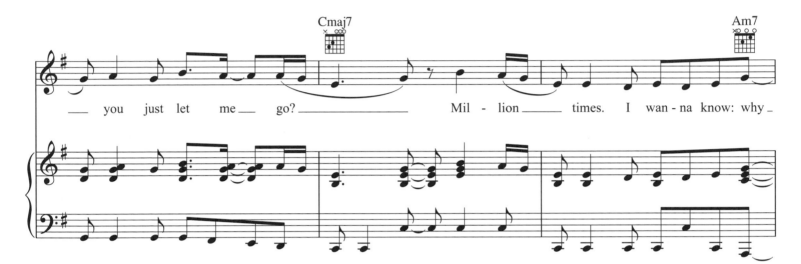

_ you just let me _ go? _____ Mil - lion _____ times. I wan - na know: why _

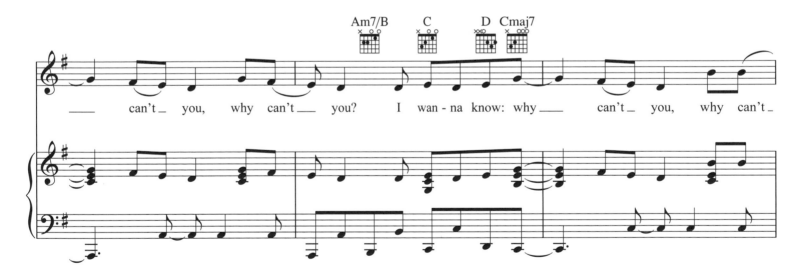

_ can't _ you, why can't _ you? I wan - na know: why ____ can't _ you, why can't _

_ you? I got - ta know: why ____ can't you, why can't ____ you just let me go? ____

STARTING OVER

Words and Music by CHRIS STAPLETON
and MIKE HENDERSON

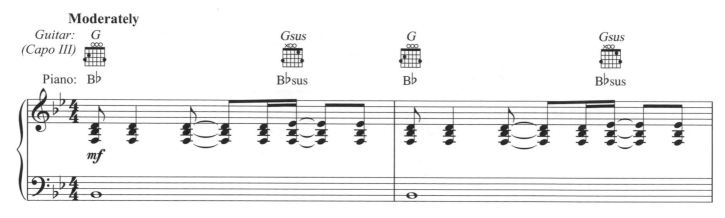

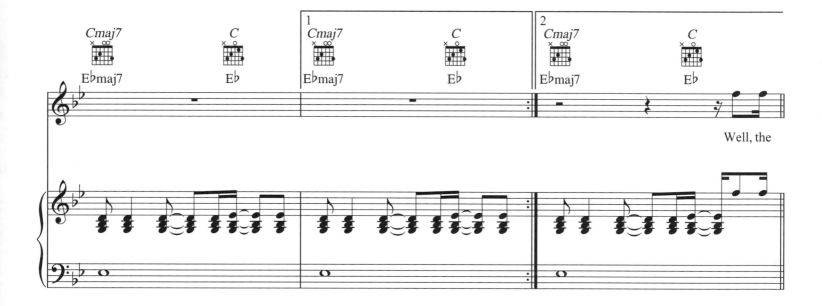

Well, the

road rolls out like a wel-come mat___ to a
might not be an___ eas-y time.___ There's

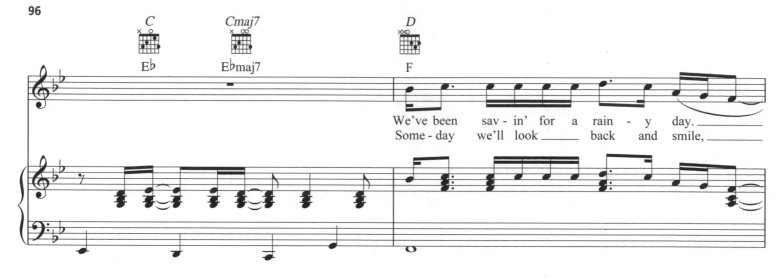

We've been sav- in' for a rain- y day. _____
Some- day we'll look _____ back and smile, _____

_____ Let's beat _ the storm _ and be on our way.)
_____ and know _ it was _ worth _ ev-'ry mile.)

And

it don't mat- ter to me; _ wher- ev- er we are _____ is where I _____ wan- na be. And,

hon- ey, for once _ in our life, let's take our chanc - es and roll _ the dice. _____

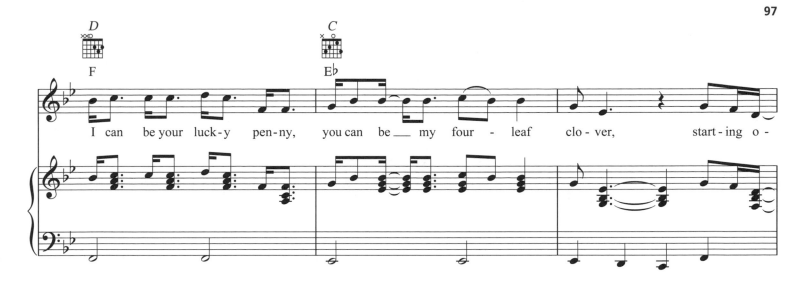

I can be your luck-y pen-ny, you can be __ my four - leaf clo - ver, start-ing o -

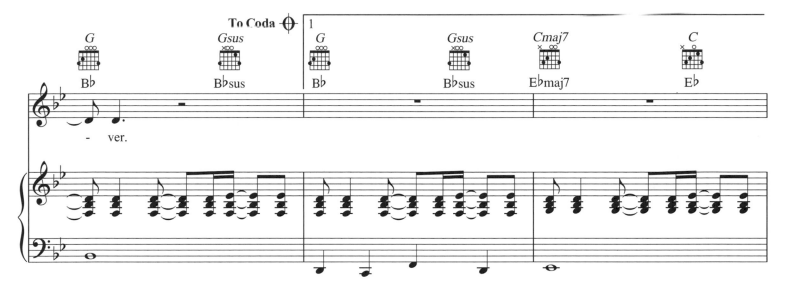

- ver.

And this

Start-ing o - ver.

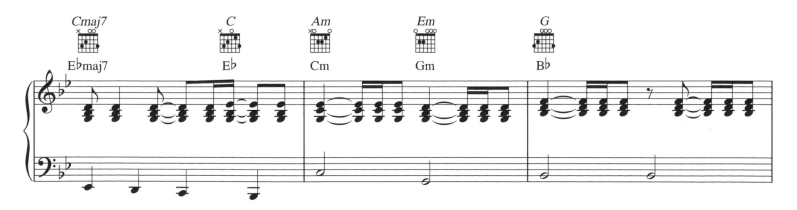

D.S. al Coda

And

Start - ing o - ver.

Ooh, _____ ooh, hoo, hoo. _

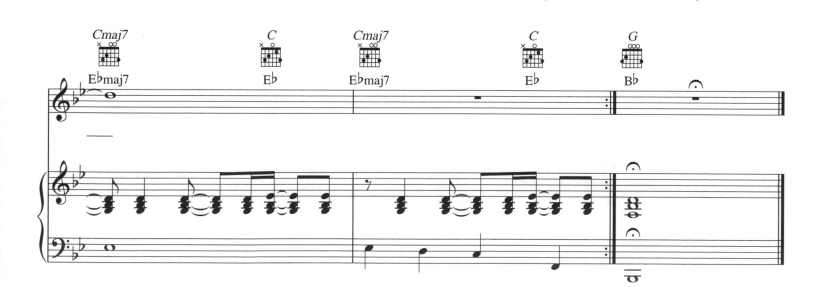

SAVAGE LOVE

Words and Music by JASON DESROULEAUX,
JOSHUA NANAI, JACOB KASHER HINDLIN
and PHILIPPE GREISS

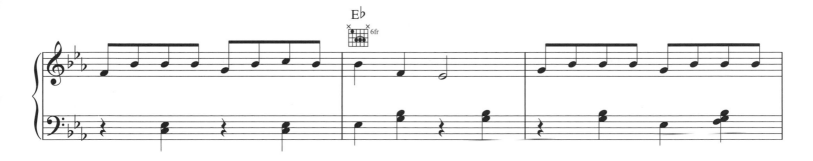

If I woke up with-out you,

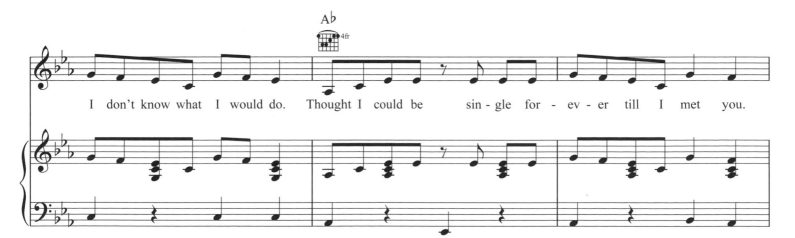

I don't know what I would do. Thought I could be sin-gle for-ev-er till I met you.

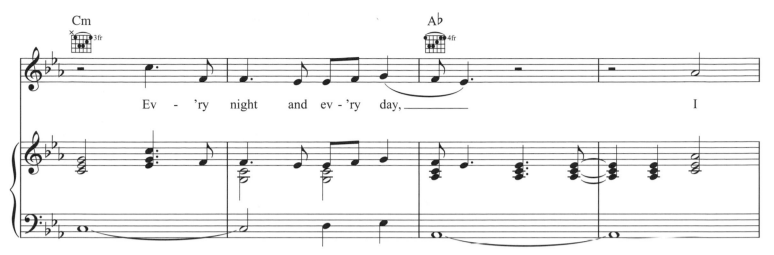

Ev - 'ry night and ev - 'ry day, _____ I

try _____ to make you stay, but ____ your... ____

Sav - age love. Did some-bod - y, did some-bod - y break your heart?

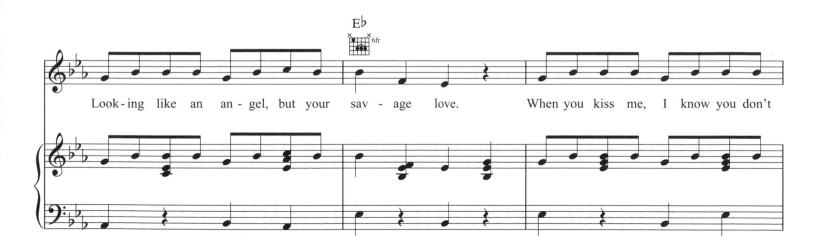

Look - ing like an an - gel, but your sav - age love. When you kiss me, I know you don't

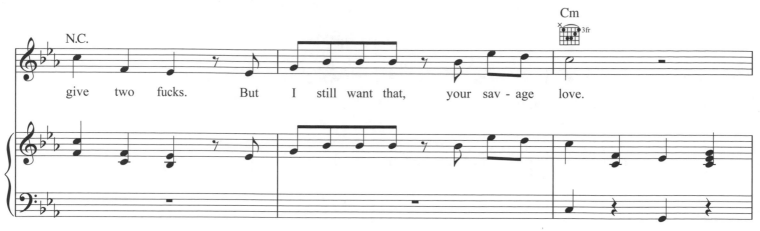

give two fucks. But I still want that, your sav - age love.

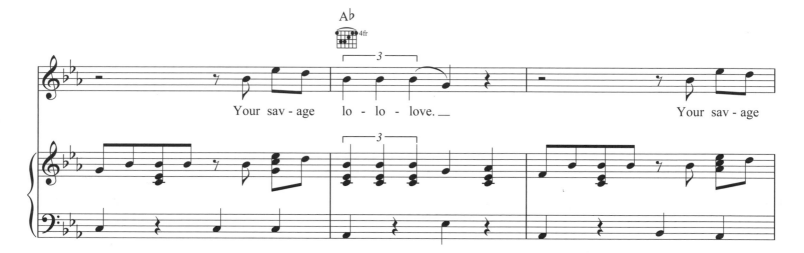

Your sav - age lo - lo - love. ___ Your sav - age

To Coda

lo - lo - love. ___ You could use ___ me ___ 'cause

1.
I still want that.

2.
I still want that, your sav - age

love. Your sav - age lo - lo - love. ___

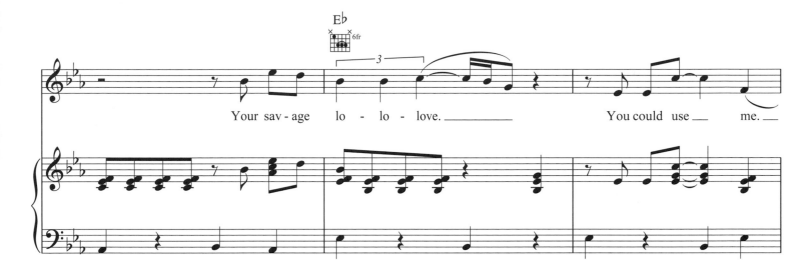

Your sav - age lo - lo - love. ___ You could use ___ me. ___

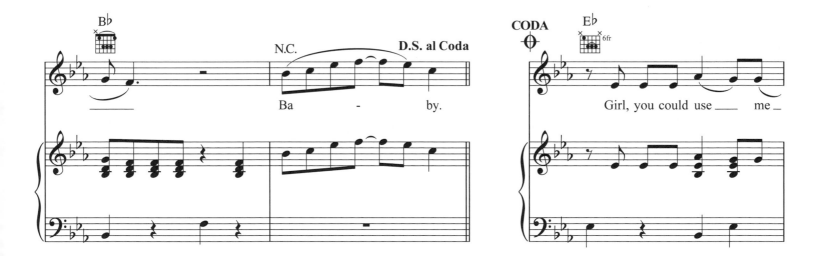

___ Ba - by. Girl, you could use ___ me ___

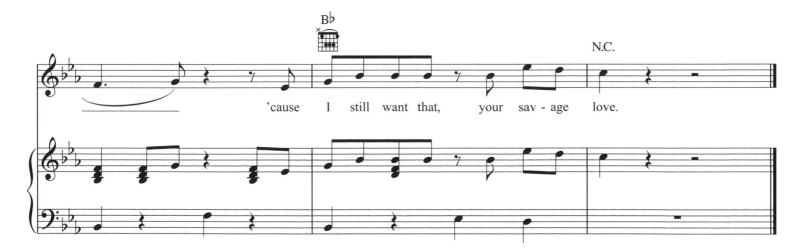

___ 'cause I still want that, your sav - age love.

THEREFORE I AM

Words and Music by BILLIE EILISH O'CONNELL
and FINNEAS O'CONNELL

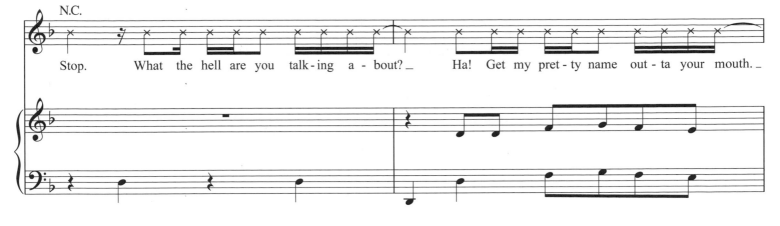

N.C.

Stop. What the hell are you talk-ing a-bout? _ Ha! Get my pret-ty name out-ta your mouth. _

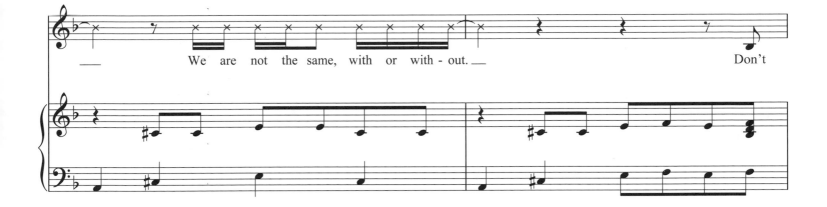

_ We are not the same, with or with-out. _ Don't

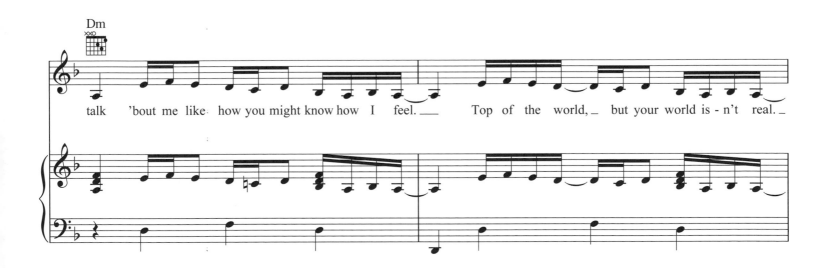

Dm

talk 'bout me like how you might know how I feel. _ Top of the world, _ but your world is-n't real. _

A

_ Your world's an i-deal. _ So, go have

fun. I real-ly could-n't care less, _ and you can give 'em my best, _ but just know, I'm not your

friend, or an-y-thing. Damn, you think that you're the

man. _ I think, there-fore I am. _ I'm not your friend, or an-y-thing.

Damn, you think that you're the man. _ I think, there-fore I am. _

D.S. al Coda

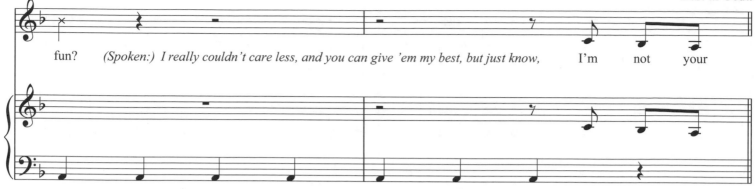

fun?   *(Spoken:) I really couldn't care less, and you can give 'em my best, but just know,*   I'm   not   your

CODA

am. ___   I'm sor - ry,   I don't think I caught your

name.   I'm ___ sor - ry,

I   don't think I caught your   name. ___

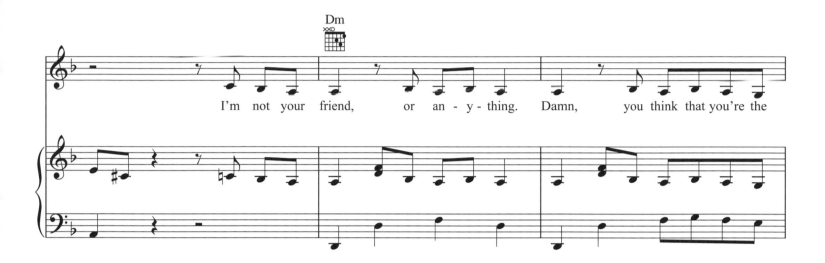

I'm not your friend, or an-y-thing. Damn, you think that you're the

man. __ I think, there-fore I am. __ I'm not your friend, or an-y-thing.

Damn, you think that you're the man. __ I think, there-fore I am. __

WILLOW

Words and Music by TAYLOR SWIFT
and AARON DESSNER

Moderately, in 2

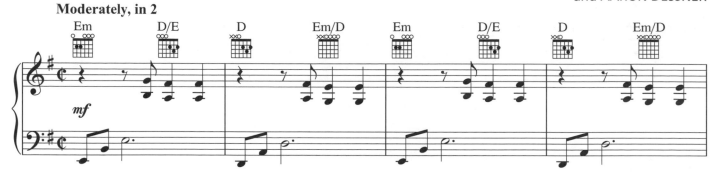

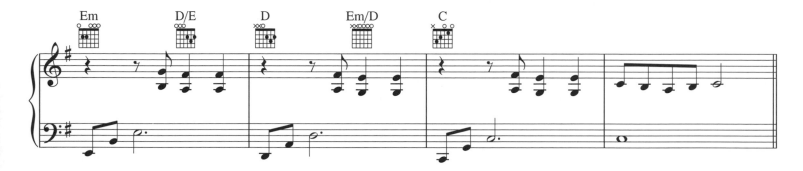

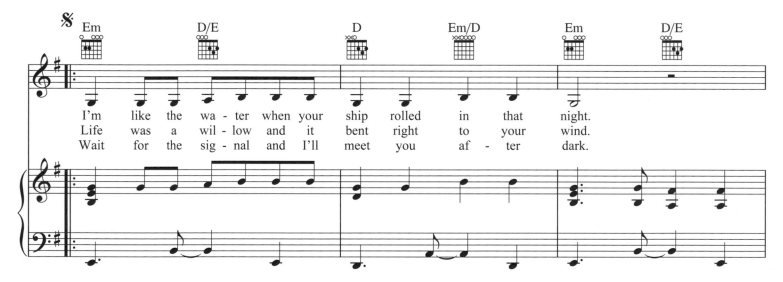

I'm like the wa- ter when your ship rolled in that night.
Life was a wil- low and it bent right to your wind.
Wait for the sig- nal and I'll meet you af- ter dark.

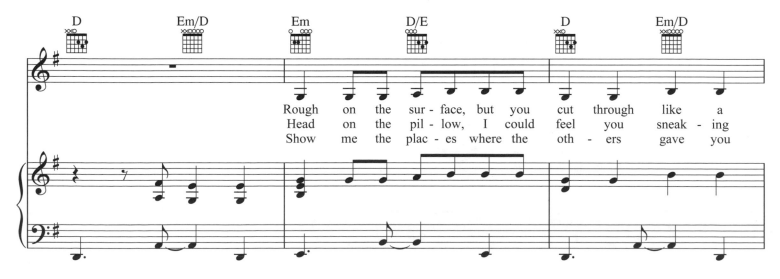

Rough on the sur- face, but you cut through like a
Head on the pil- low, I could feel you sneak- ing
Show me the plac- es where the oth- ers gave you

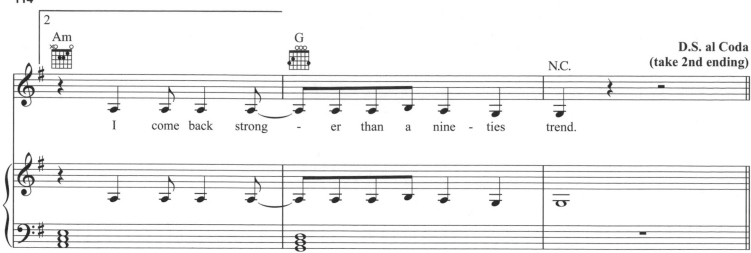

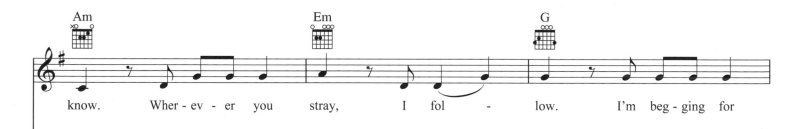

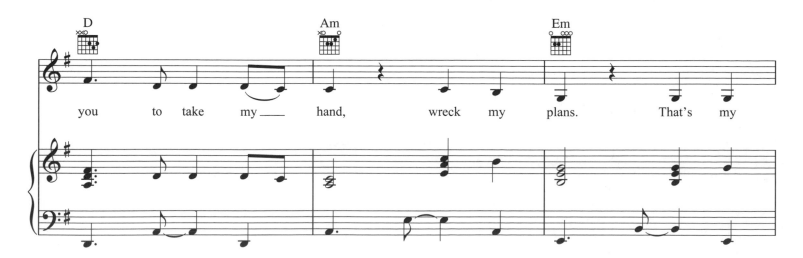

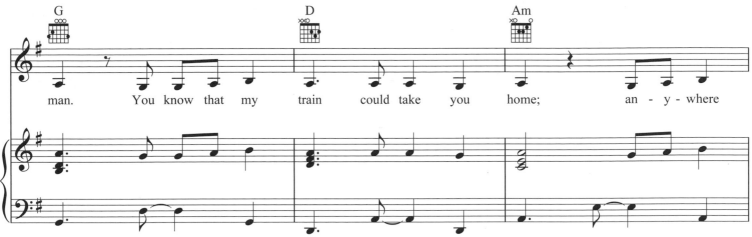

man. You know that my train could take you home; an-y-where

else is hol - low. I'm beg-ging for you to take my

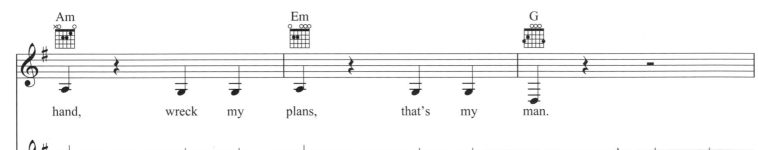

hand, wreck my plans, that's my man.

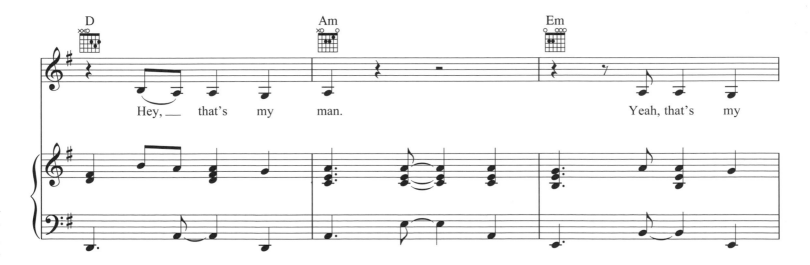

Hey, __ that's my man. Yeah, that's my

man.   Yeah, that's my   man.   Ev - 'ry bait and

switch   was   a   work   of   art.   That's   my   man.

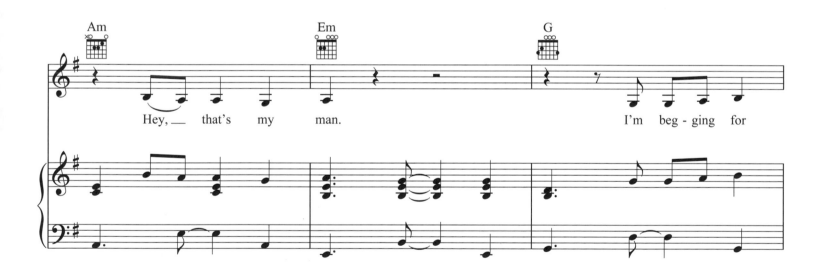

Hey, ___ that's   my   man.   I'm   beg - ging   for

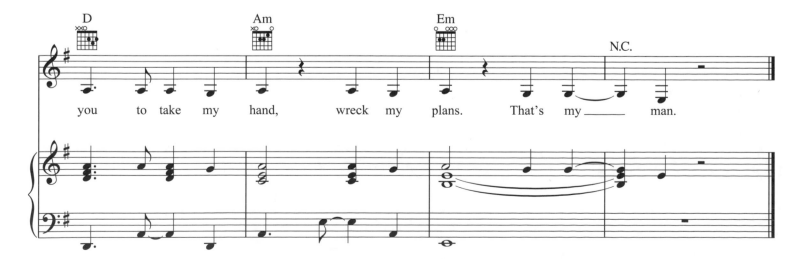

you   to   take   my   hand,   wreck   my   plans.   That's   my ___ man.

WATERMELON SUGAR

Words and Music by HARRY STYLES,
THOMAS HULL, MITCHELL ROWLAND
and TYLER JOHNSON

Moderate groove

Tastes like straw-ber-ries on a sum-mer eve-ning,
Straw-ber-ries on a sum-mer eve-ning;

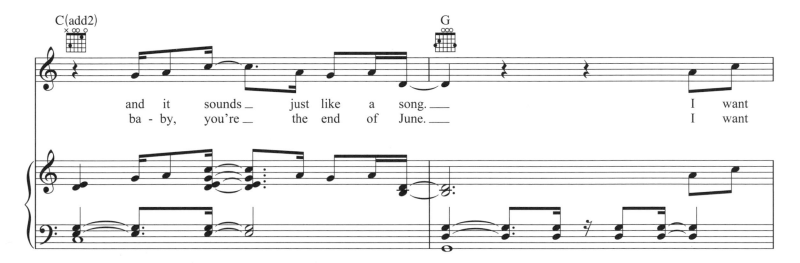

and it sounds just like a song.
ba-by, you're the end of June.
I want
I want

more ber-ries and that sum-mer feel-ing.
your bel-ly and that sum-mer feel-ing,

It's so won - der - ful and warm. ⎤
get - ting washed _ a - way in you. ⎦ Breathe me _ in, _

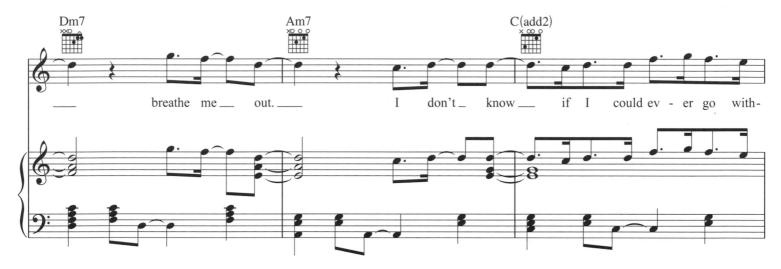

_ breathe me _ out. _ I don't _ know _ if I could ev - er go with-

Omit 2nd Time

out. I'm _ just think - ing _ out loud. I _ don't

know if I could ev - er go with - out wa - ter - mel - on sug - ar

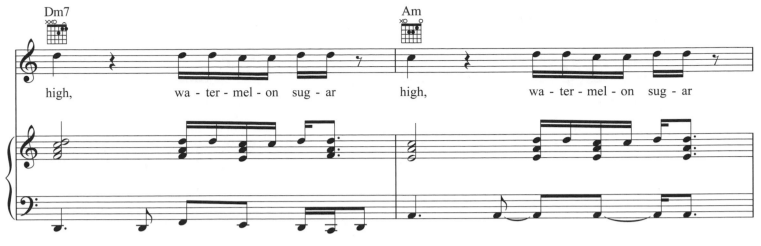

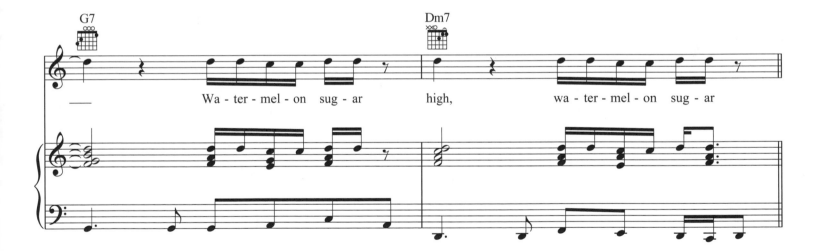

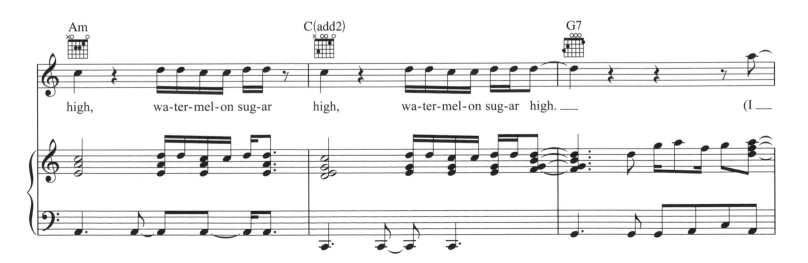

just wan-na taste it, I just wan-na taste it, wa - ter-mel-on sug - ar high.)

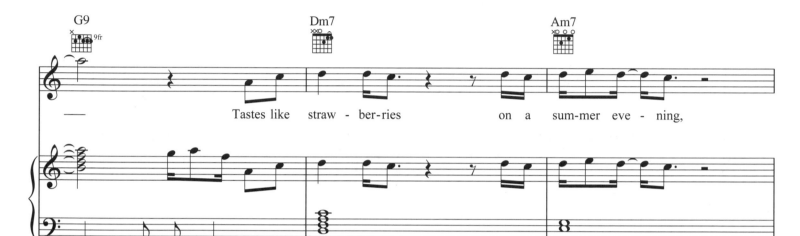

Tastes like straw-ber-ries on a sum-mer eve - ning,

and it sounds just like a song. I want your bel - ly and that

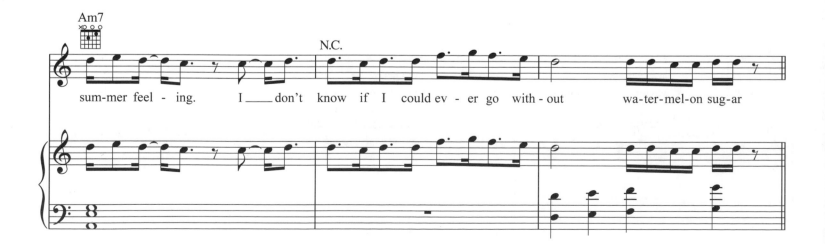

sum-mer feel - ing. I don't know if I could ev-er go with-out wa-ter-mel-on sug-ar

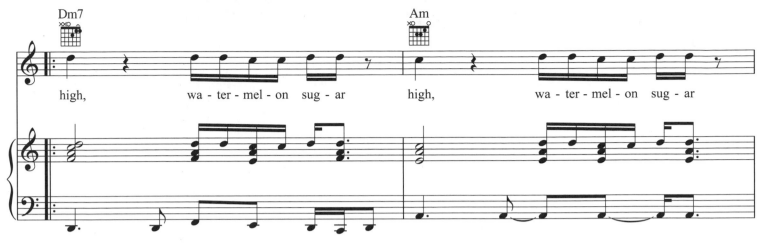

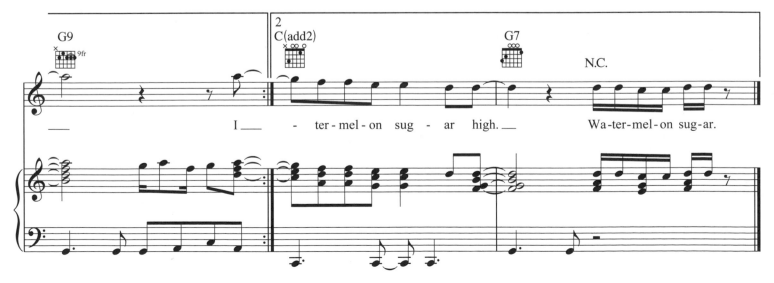

YOU BROKE ME FIRST

Words and Music by TATE McRAE,
BLAKE HARNAGE and VICTORIA ZARO

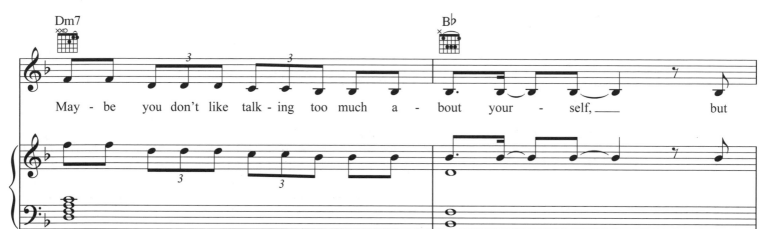

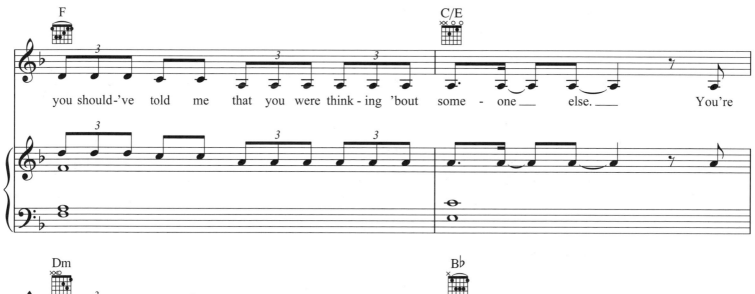

Recorded a half step lower.

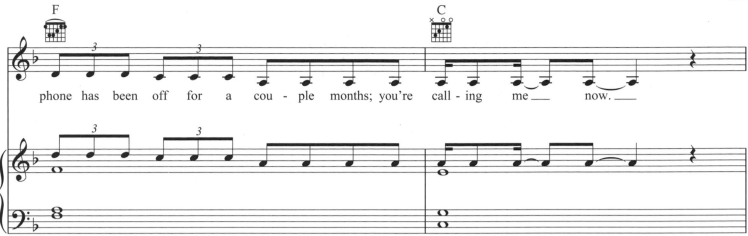

phone has been off for a cou-ple months; you're call-ing me___ now.___

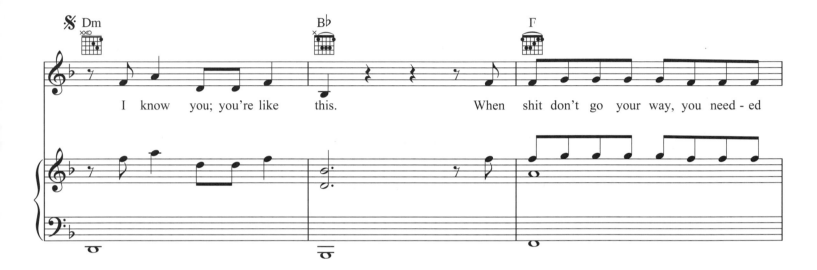

I know you; you're like this. When shit don't go your way, you need-ed

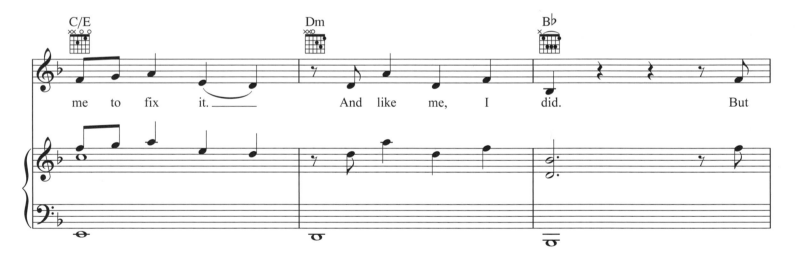

me to fix it.___ And like me, I did. But

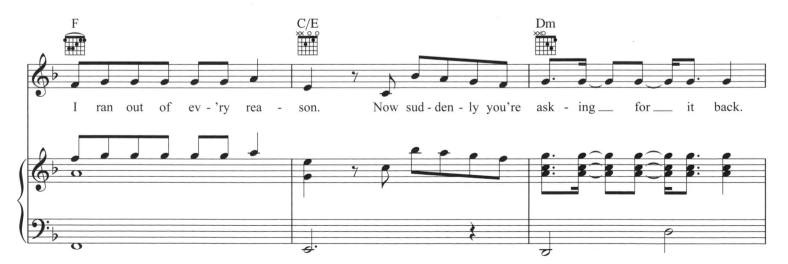

I ran out of ev-'ry rea-son. Now sud-den-ly you're ask-ing___ for___ it back.

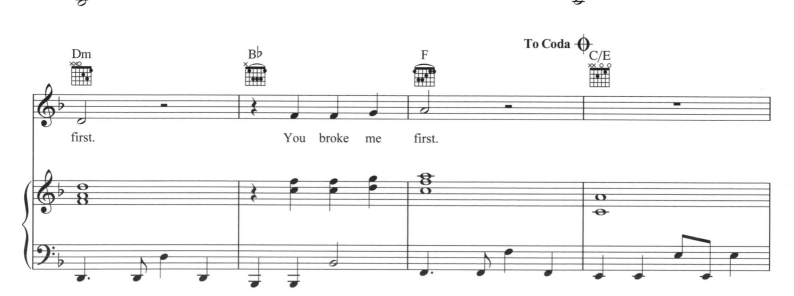

Took a while, was in de - ni - al when I first ___ heard ___ that

you moved on quick - er than I could have ev - er; you know that ___ hurt. ___

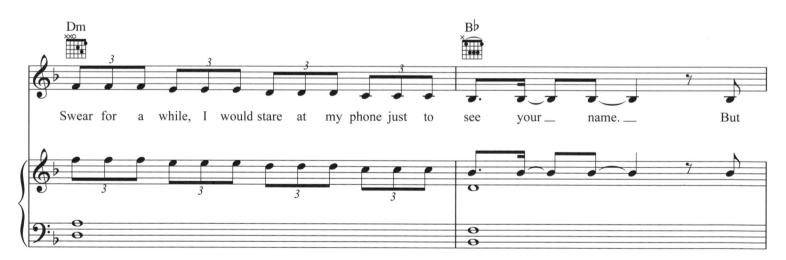

Swear for a while, I would stare at my phone just to see your ___ name. ___ But

D.S. al Coda

now that it's there, I don't real - ly know what to say.

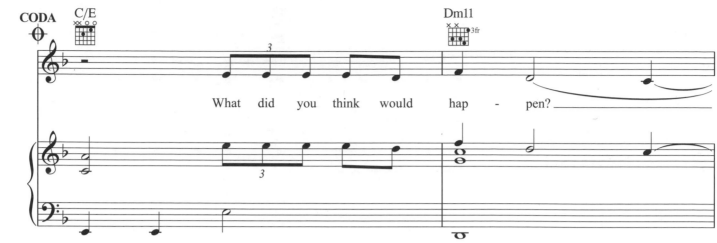

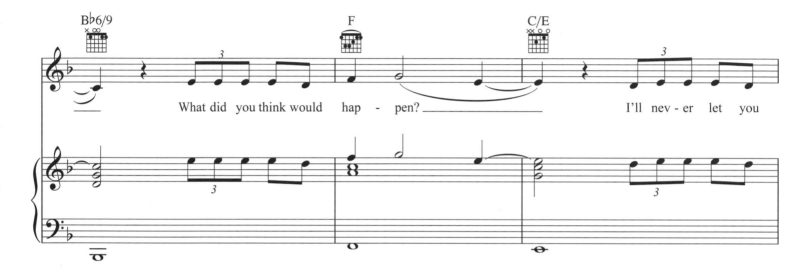

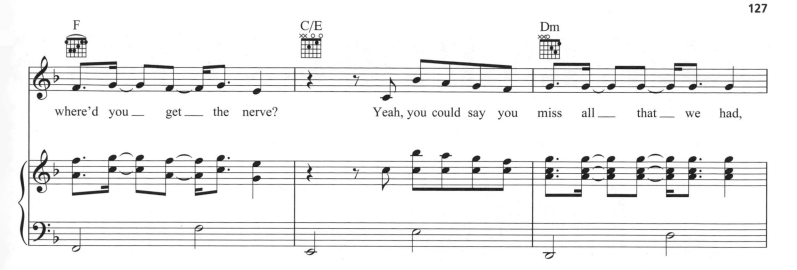

where'd you __ get __ the nerve?   Yeah, you could say you miss all __ that __ we had,

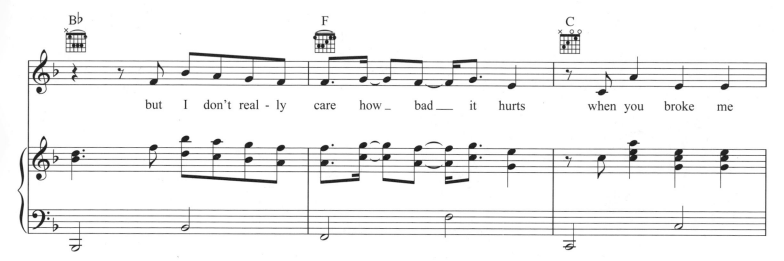

but I don't real-ly care how __ bad __ it hurts   when you broke me

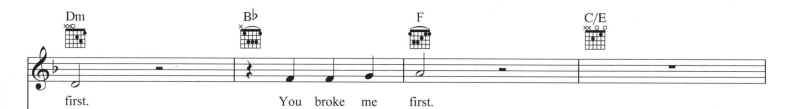

first.   You broke me   first.

You broke me   first.   Ah. _____

CONTEMPORARY HITS
FOR PIANO, VOICE AND GUITAR